TABLE OF CONTENTS

FAVORITE AIR FRYER RECIPES...36

SNACKS & APPETIZERS RECIPES 47

BREAKFAST & BRUNCH RECIPES 57

SANDWICHES & BURGERS RECIPES 104

INTRODUCTION

WHAT FOODS ARE BEST FOR THE AIR FRYER?

Now that you have decided on the best air fryer for you, the fun part is actually putting it to use! You can pretty much put any food into your air fryer to cook however, just like other kitchen appliances, there are certain foods that cook better than others. I have noted of what works best in the air fryer after trying out different recipes and here are my findings.

FROZEN FOODS

The original concept of the air fryer was made to reheat and rapidly cook frozen foods. I found that it does this well. All the food was cooked to perfection with no oil added. The food was cooked right through without any burning on the outside. Some of the frozen foods that I cooked and the results:

- French fries: Comes out crispier and crunchier than the oven.
- Mini pizza's: Toppings are juicy and the base is crunchy.
- Chicken nuggets: Outer layer is crispy and chicken inside is tender.
- Vegetable croquettes: Crispy on the outside and soft on the inside.
- Meatballs: Outer layer is crispy and meat inside is tender.
- Chicken wings: Perfectly grilled on the outside and juicy on the inside.
- Fish sticks: Crunchy on the outside and soft on the inside.
- Chicken breasts: Soft and tender on the inside.
- Fish fillets: Melts in your mouth.

The only thing to be aware of is that smaller air fryers might not fit a medium to large size pizzas. Therefore you need to consider what types of food you will be cooking regularly when deciding on your air fryer size.

VEGETABLES

Most of the vegetables that you love can be cooked in the air fryer. However, depending on how you like you like them done, some vegetables are better in the air fryer than others.

It was noted that some vegetables comes out soft and juicy while others comes out crispy and crunchy. I also noticed that they do seem to retain more of their nutritional value as the vegetables were not overcooked.

Soft and juicy vegetables when air fried included:
- Mushrooms
- Zucchini
- Butternut squash
- Cherry tomatoes
- Aubergine
- Bell Pepper

Crispy and crunchy vegetables when air fried included:
- Cauliflower
- Brussels sprouts
- Asparagus

Vegetables that I am still trying to perfect with the air fryer:
- Broccoli: They are too crunchy for me and when I tried to increase the time, they get a bit burnt.
- Sweet Potato: The outside gets a bit burnt if I want the inside cooked through.

MEATS

Cooking meat with the air fryer is a delight as you don't have to worry about the meat being burnt or undercooked, especially uneven pieces of meat. The only trick is to get the right temperature and timer set to have a perfectly cooked piece of meat. The first step would be the user manual of your air fryer. Then you can refer to any cookbooks or any other recipes that you can come across. Some air fryers even have preset programs that you can use as a beginner. Once you have got an estimated temperature or timer you can manually adjust the elements up or down to suit the way you like to have your meat. As we all have different taste buds and preferences, it may take you a few tries before you find your perfect settings. In saying this, I have listed below some of my findings while cooking my meat in the air fryer.

Chicken: With the small air fryers the best chicken pieces to cook would be the evenly shaped pieces like chicken breasts and chicken tenderloins as the basket size is smaller. The family sized and extra large air fryers can accommodate a whole chicken depending on the model and capacity air fryer you have. Chicken generally comes out tender and juicy.

- *Beef*: Steaks and kebabs are done fairly well as it can be done medium to well done simply by adjusting the temperature or timer settings. You have control of the process. Most air fryers even allows you to slide the basket out during the cooking process to check on your food midway.
- *Lamb*: Steaks and lamb chops are done perfectly when air fried as they are juicy and tender. Lamb rack , however, proved to be tricky depending on the size of your air fryer. For small to medium air fryers it is recommended to cut it into smaller pieces for best results.

SEAFOOD

I found grilling seafood in the air fryer keeps most of the juices inside therefore I could taste more of the seafood flavor. Naturally, fresh seafood is always best if you want to taste the seafood flavors.

I found that seafood is cooked faster in the air fryer and the flesh is soft and tender. Some of the things to note are:

- Prawns and Lobster: Grilling them in the shell really brought out there natural flavors.
- Fish: Fillets had the best outcome with the air fryer as they fit in the basket and there is still enough room for the air circulation to cook them evenly. Even with salmon fillets where the middle are thicker and the edges are thinner, the air fryer is able to cook them evenly. Grilling whole fish is also great in the bigger air fryers but not recommended for smaller air fryers as you would need to cut your fish in half.
- Scallops: Few minutes in the air fryer and they come out tender, juicy and full of flavor.

You can put most food types into the air fryer for cooking. The trick is to get the settings right for each specific type of food. This comes with trying different recipes and noting down what you like and don't like. Over time, you would have discovered what works best to suit your taste buds. Hope that you can have as much fun as I am cooking with air fryer!

BEEF, PORK & LAMB RECIPES

Easy Pork Dumplings

Servings: 48

Ingredients:

- DUMPLINGS
- 4 hot or sweet Italian sausages, casings removed
- 4 scallions, finely chopped
- 3 tablespoons chopped fresh cilantro
- 1 large egg, beaten
- 1 tablespoon soy sauce
- 1 tablespoon grated fresh ginger (from a 2-in. piece)
- 1 teaspoon toasted sesame oil
- 48 round wonton wrappers (from a 14-oz. pkg.)
- Vegetable oil, for cooking
- DIPPING SAUCE
- 2 tablespoons soy sauce
- 1 tablespoon rice vinegar
- 1 scallion, thinly sliced
- 1 teaspoon granulated sugar
- 1 teaspoon toasted sesame oil

Directions:

1. Make The Dumplings Line A Large Baking Sheet With Parchment Paper. Using A Fork, Stir Together Sausage, Scallions, Cilantro, Egg, Soy Sauce, Ginger, And Sesame Oil In A Large Bowl. Fill A Small Bowl With Water. Lay 3 Wonton Wrappers On A Work Surface. Place 1 Rounded Teaspoon Of Sausage Mixture In The Center Of Each Wrapper. Dip A Finger In Water And Rub Around The Edge Of Each Wrapper. Fold 1 Side Of Wrapper Over Filling. Make 3 Pleats Along Seam And Pinch To Seal. Transfer Assembled Dumplings To Prepared Baking Sheet. Repeat With Remaining Sausage Mixture And Wrappers.Add Water To A Medium Nonstick Skillet Until Bottom Is Just Covered; Bring To A Simmer Over Medium-High. Add As Many Dumplings, Flat Side Down, As Will Comfortably Fit. Cover And Steam Until Wrappers Are Translucent, About 3 Minutes.Pour Off Any Water Remaining In Skillet. Add 2 Tablespoons Vegetable Oil (If Dumplings Are Sticking, Shake Skillet Gently Or Loosen Dumplings With A Rubber Spatula).

Cook, Undisturbed, Until Bottoms Are Golden And Crispy, About 1 Minute. Transfer Dumplings To A Paper Towel– Lined Plate. Wipe Skillet Clean And Repeat With Water, Remaining Dumplings, And Vegetable Oil.

2. Make The Dipping Sauces Tir Together All Ingredients Plus 1 Tablespoon Water In A Small Bowl Until Sugar Dissolves. Serve With Dumplings

3. To Freezet Ransfer Uncooked Dumplings On Baking Sheet To Freezer. Freeze, Uncovered, Until Firm, About 2 Hours. Remove Frozen Dumplings From Baking Sheet And Transfer To A Resealable Plastic Bag. Freeze For Up To 3 Months. Cook As Directed (Do Not Thaw), Adding 2 To 3 Minutes To Steam Time.

Air Fryer Country-style Ribs

Servings: 4-5

Cooking Time: 20 Minutes

Ingredients:

- 2 pounds country-style boneless pork ribs
- 1 ½ teaspoons smoked paprika
- ½ teaspoon kosher salt
- ½ teaspoon black pepper
- ½ teaspoon garlic powder
- ¼ teaspoon onion powder
- ¼ teaspoon cayenne pepper
- 1 cup BBQ sauce

Directions:

1. Preheat an air fryer to 370 degrees F. Combine the paprika, salt, pepper, garlic powder, onion powder, and cayenne in a small bowl and set aside.
2. Trim the ribs, if necessary, and spray or rub them with cooking oil, then sprinkle the ribs with the seasoning, massaging in it on all sides.
3. Place the country-style ribs in the air fryer in an even layer. Cook for 20 minutes, flipping once halfway through at the 10-minute mark.
4. When the timer goes off, brush them with a thin layer of BBQ sauce, then place them back in the basket and cook for 5-8 more minutes.
5. Serve with additional BBQ sauce.

Notes

HOW TO COOK FROZEN COUNTRY-STYLE RIBS IN THE AIR FRYER:

Prepare the ribs through step 2, then freeze in a plastic zipper bag.

When ready to cook, spray the inside of the air fryer basket with non-stick spray. Place the frozen ribs inside in a single layer. Cook at 380 degrees F for 20 minutes, flipping once more halfway through the cooking time at the 10-minute mark.

When the timer goes off, remove the ribs from the fryer. Brush the ribs with a thin layer of BBQ sauce, then place them back in the basket and cook for 8-10 more minutes at 400 degrees F.

Serve with additional BBQ sauce.

HOW TO REHEAT COUNTRY-STYLE RIBS IN THE AIR FRYER:

Spray the inside of the air fryer basket, then place the ribs inside. Air fry at 380 for 5 minutes, until warmed through.

Serve with additional BBQ sauce.

Air Fryer Bacon-wrapped Figs

Servings: 12

Cooking Time: 10 Minutes

Ingredients:

- 12 dried Turkish or mission figs
- 6 strips regular center-cut bacon (not thick cut)
- Goat cheese or blue cheese for stuffing, optional
- Salted, roasted almonds for stuffing, optional
- Honey, for serving
- Nonstick spray, for air fryer

Directions:

1. Reconstitute the figs:
2. Add the dried figs to a bowl filled with steaming hot water. Let them sit for 20 minutes to reconstitute. Drain the figs and cut off the stems. Cut a small slit in each fig and spoon in a little blue cheese or goat cheese, or half an almond, if desired. You could also do a mix of fillings.
3. Wrap the bacon around the figs:
4. Cut the strips of bacon in half and trim them down to about 1/2 to 3/4 inches wide. Wrap one bacon strip around each fig. Secure with a toothpick.
5. Air fry the figs:

6. Spray the basket of your air fryer with nonstick spray. Add bacon-wrapped figs in a single layer so they aren't touching. Air fry the figs at 350 F for 8-9 minutes, flipping once halfway through.
7. If you don't have an air fryer, broil the figs on high for about 3 minutes per side.
8. Serve the figs:
9. Once the figs have cooled slightly, serve them drizzled with honey.
10. Leftover figs (yeah right!) will keep in the fridge for up to 5 days. Reheat in a 350 F oven, or reheat in the air fryer for a few minutes before eating.

Air Fryer Pork Belly Bites

Servings: 4

Cooking Time: 15 Minutes

Ingredients:

- 1 lb. (454 g) pork belly , rinsed & patted dry
- 1 teaspoon (5 ml) Worcestershire sauce or soy sauce
- 1/2 teaspoon (2.5 ml) garlic powder
- salt , to taste
- black pepper , to taste
- 1/4 cup BBQ sauce (optional)(sugar-free bbq sauce is a nice low-carb option)

Directions:

1. Preheat the Air Fryer at 400°F for 4 minutes. This will give the pork bites a really good sear.
2. If needed, remove the skin from the pork belly. Cut the pork belly into 3/4"□ sized cubes and place in a bowl. Season with Worcestershire sauce, garlic powder, salt and pepper. Spread the pork belly in even layer in air fryer basket.
3. Air Fry at 400°F for 10-18 minutes, shaking and flipping and the pork belly 2 times through cooking process (time depends on your preferred doneness, thickness of the pork belly, size & cooking intensity of your air fryer).
4. If you want it more done, add an extra 2-5 minutes of cooking time. Check the pork belly to see how well done it is cooked.
5. Season with additional salt & pepper if desired. It needs a good amount of seasoning to bring out the flavors. Drizzle with optional bbq sauce if desired. Serve warm.

Notes

If using a large air fryer, the recipe might cook quicker so adjust cooking time.

If cooking in multiple batches (if you have a small air fryer or are doubling the recipe), the first batch will take longer to cook if Air Fryer is not already pre-heated.

Remember to set a timer to shake/flip/toss the food as directed in recipe.

Vortex Air Fryer Pork Belly Bites

Servings: 6 -8

Cooking Time: 12 - 15 Minutes

Ingredients:
- 1 kg pork belly
- 2 Tbls brown sugar
- 1 ? Tbls smoked paprika
- 1 tsp garlic powder
- Pinch salt
- Black pepper
- Olive oil cooking spray
- Sauce:
- 2 Tbls brown sugar
- ? cup barbeque sauce
- 3 Tbls honey
- 1 Tbls soya sauce

Directions:
1. Cut the pork belly into 5 cm square pieces.
2. Mix the sugar, paprika, garlic powder, salt & pepper together.
3. Toss the pork in the dry rub mix.
4. Place uncovered in a bowl in the fridge for 1 hour.
5. This allows to pork to dry out and therefore become crispy.
6. Place the pieces onto the Vortex / Duo Crisp baking trays and spray each piece with the olive oil spray.
7. Bake at 200C for 12 C 15 mins, turning halfway through cooking.
8. Remove from the vortex oven and toss in the sauce.
9. To make the sauce add the ingredients to a saucepan and slowly bring to the boil.
10. Garnish with fresh coriander and sliced chilli.

Air Fryer Steak

Servings: 2

Cooking Time: 10 Minutes

Ingredients:
- 1-2 tablespoons steak seasoning
- 1 tablespoon kosher salt
- 1 tablespoon freshly cracked ground black pepper
- 1 teaspoon garlic powder
- 1 teaspoon light brown sugar
- ½ teaspoon red pepper flakes
- 1 1 lb. ribeye or New York strip steak
- 1 tablespoon olive oil

Directions:
1. Season the steak with 1 tablespoon of steak seasoning (or more if you would like) and massage the seasoning into both sides of the steak. Let the steak sit at room temperature for 15 minutes.
2. Preheat the air fryer to 400°F drizzle ½ tablespoon of olive oil in the bottom of the air fryer.
3. Transfer the steak to the air fryer and drizzle with the rest of the olive oil. Cook for 10 minutes, flipping halfway through.
4. When the steak reaches 135°F (for medium rare) remove the steak from the air fryer and let it rest for 10 minutes before slicing.

Notes

This recipe has been tested with both a New York strip and a ribeye steak. Both work great.

The larger the cut of meat, the longer you need to cook the steak.This recipe has been tested with and without seasoning. The seasoning helps to add a delicious crust to the outside of the steak.

Steak Internal Temperatures135°F – rare140°F – medium rare150°F – medium165°F – well-done

Air Fryer Pork Tenderloin

Servings: 6

Cooking Time: 15 Minutes

Ingredients:

- 1 1/2 lbs pork tenderloin
- 1/2 teaspoon salt
- 1/2 teaspoon pepper
- 2 tablespoons olive oil
- 1 teaspoon dijon mustard
- 1 teaspoon honey
- 1 teaspoon garlic powder
- 1 teaspoon smoked paprika
- 1/2 teaspoon chili optional

Directions:

1. Season the pork with salt and pepper.
2. In a small bowl, whisk the remaining ingredients. Coat the exterior of the pork tenderloin with it.
3. Add the pork into an air fryer basket and air fry at 200F/400F for 15 minutes, flipping halfway through.
4. The pork tenderloin is fully cooked when it reaches an internal temperature opf 145F.
5. Let the pork rest for 5 minutes before slicing and serving.

Notes

TO STORE: Place leftovers in an airtight container and store it in the refrigerator for up to five days.

TO FREEZE: Place the cooked and cooled tenderloin in a ziplock bag and store it in the freezer for up to 6 months.

TO REHEAT: You can reheat in the air fryer, oven or skillet.

Katsu Curry

Servings: 4

Ingredients:

- For the Katsu sauce
- 2 tbsp olive oil
- 1 onion, diced
- 2 carrots, peeled and chopped
- 2 stalks celery, finely sliced
- 4 garlic cloves, peeled and sliced
- 2 thumbs ginger, peeled and chopped
- 1 pink lady apple, chopped
- 2 heaped tbsp curry powder
- 1/2 tsp turmeric powder
- 1/2 tsp ginger
- 1/2 tsp cinnamon
- 1 1/2 tsp sea salt
- 400ml can coconut milk
- 400ml water
- 2 tbsp maple syrup
- 2 tbsp rice vinegar
- 2 tbsp tamari sauce
- For the breaded aubergine & tofu
- 1 medium aubergine
- 400g block tofu
- 6 tbsp flour
- 2 eggs, beaten
- 16 tbsp breadcrumbs
- 1/2 tsp sea salt
- 2 tbsp olive oil or cooking spray
- For the chips
- 4 baking potatoes
- 2 tbsp olive oil
- 1/4 tsp sea salt
- To serve
- Baby gem lettuce
- Lime
- Pickles chillies

Directions:

1. To make the katsu curry sauce; heat the olive oil in a saucepan over a medium heat. Once warm, add the diced onion, carrot and celery and sauté for 8 minutes

2. Add the garlic, ginger and apple and continue frying for a further 4 mins. Stir often

3. Next add the curry powder, turmeric, ground ginger, ground cinnamon and sea salt. Stir and sauté for 2 mins

4. Finally add the coconut milk, water, maple syrup, rice vinegar, tamari sauce and stir well. Bring to a gentle simmer, and cook over a low/medium heat with the lid off for 25-30 mins

5. Allow to cool before blending sauce until smooth and glossy. This will reheat perfectly when you are ready to serve

6. To prepare breaded aubergine and tofu; slice the aubergine into 1cm thick rounds, and cut the tofu into 1cm assorted shapes

7. Prepare three bowls to 'bread' the katsu pieces – one with flour, one with beaten egg, and one with seasoned bread crumbs

8. Work piece by piece to dip each one in flour, then egg, and lastly in breadcrumbs. Note, the aubergine will need a 'double dip'. Spray or brush pieces with oil

9. Place crisper plates in both drawers. Place katsu in Zone 1 drawer, select AIR FRY, set temperature to 180°C and time to 15 minutes

10. Slice potatoes into chunky chips, toss with olive oil and sea salt, and place in Zone 2 drawer, select AIR FRY, set temperature to 200°C and time to 18 minutes. Select SYNC. Select START/STOP to begin

11. After 9 minutes, open drawers and shake or turn food around

12. When cooking is complete, pile golden chips, crispy Katsu pieces onto plates and top with hot katsu curry sauce. Serve with lettuce, a squeeze of lime and some pickled chillies

Italian Pork Loin & Roasted Vegetables

Servings: 6

Ingredients:

- 1 uncooked boneless pork tenderloin (675-900g), cut in half widthwise
- 120ml Italian dressing
- 1 aubergine, peeled, cut in 2.5cm pieces
- 2 plum tomatoes, diced
- 1 courgette, sliced in half moons
- 1 medium red onion, peeled and cut in 2.5cm pieces
- 1 red bell pepper, diced
- 3 cloves of garlic, peeled, minced
- 2 tbsp extra virgin olive oil
- 30g fresh basil, torn
- 2 tbsp salt, divided

Directions:

1. Place pork loin into a bowl. Coat pork with Italian dressing. Cover and refrigerate for 2 to 4 hours.

2. In a large bowl, toss aubergine, tomatoes, courgette, red onion and garlic with oil, basil, and 1 tablespoon salt.

3. Insert crisper plate in pan and pan in unit. Preheat unit by selecting ROAST, setting temperature to 190°C and setting time to 3 minutes. Select START/STOP to begin.

4. While unit is preheating, remove pork from marinade and season with remaining 1 tablespoon salt.

5. Once the unit is preheated, place vegetable mixture on the crisper plate. Place pork on top of vegetables.

6. Select ROAST, set temperature to 190°C, and set time to 20 minutes. Select START/STOP to begin.

7. After 10 minutes, remove pan. Stir vegetables and flip the pork. Reinsert pan to resume cooking.

8. When cooking is complete, let pork rest for 5 minutes before slicing.

Air Fryer Bacon

Servings: 2

Cooking Time: 5 Minutes

Ingredients:
- 4 strips bacon thick or thin, cut in half crosswise
- Black pepper optional

Directions:
1. Wipe out your air fryer to avoid bacon smoking. Preheat the air fryer to 350 degrees F. If you'd like to keep the bacon warm between batches, preheat your oven to 250 degrees F.
2. Slide out your air fryer basket. With tongs, arrange the halved bacon slices in a single layer. Make sure they do not overlap (a little bit of touching at the edges is OK). If desired, sprinkle with black pepper. Depending upon the size of your basket and the number of strips you'd like to cook at once, you may need to cook the bacon in batches.
3. Cook the bacon for 5 minutes (for thinner bacon) or up to 9 minutes (for thicker bacon), until it reaches your desired crispness. The bacon will curl as it crisps. Check the bacon's progress frequently to make sure it doesn't burn.
4. Transfer the bacon to a paper towel-lined plate and lightly blot. If desired, transfer the bacon to a baking sheet and keep in the oven.
5. For further batches: Repeat with remaining bacon (no need to wipe out the air fryer in between unless it begins to smoke, in which case carefully pour out the grease and wipe it with a paper towel). Enjoy!

Notes

If the bacon begins to smoke, this is likely old grease that was left in your air fryer (as long as your air fryer is set to less than 360 degrees F, it should not smoke). Once your air fryer is cool, wipe it out with a damp cloth to prevent further smoking. I have also read you can place a slice of bread in the air fryer basket when making bacon to absorb excess grease and prevent smoke.

TO STORE: Refrigerate bacon strips in an airtight storage container for up to 2 days.

TO REHEAT: Recrisp bacon in the air fryer at 350 degrees F.

TO FREEZE: Freeze bacon strips in an airtight freezer-safe storage container or ziptop bag. Reheat from frozen as desired.

Air Fryer Bacon Wrapped Corn Dogs

Servings: 4

Cooking Time: 10 Minutes

Ingredients:
- 4 slices bacon
- 4 corn dogs

Directions:
1. Remove the corn dogs from the freezer.
2. Take a slice of bacon and carefully wrap the entire corn dog.
3. Place the bacon wrapped corn dogs in a single layer into the basket of the air fryer.
4. Air fry the corn dogs at 370 degrees Fahrenheit for 9-10 minutes, or until the bacon is cooked and crispy.
5. Carefully remove the corn dogs from the air fryer basket and serve them on a plate with your favorite dipping sauce.

Notes

I use one piece of thin sliced bacon for each of my regular sized corn dogs. If you want the entire corn dog to be covered in bacon, Use two pieces and allow them to overlap slightly when you're applying the bacon to the corn dog. This will allow for the shrinkage that occurs during the cooking process.

I use a 5.8qt Cosori air fryer and I find that 10 minutes is the perfect amount of cook time for one pieces of bacon. If you are completely covering the corn dog with two pieces of bacon and over lapping pieces, you may need to add an additional minute or two to reach your desired level of crispness.

Crispy Air Fryer Bacon

Servings: 5

Cooking Time: 9 Minutes

Ingredients:

- 5 slices bacon , (6 oz regular bacon, or 8-12 oz thick-cut bacon)

Directions:

1. Place the bacon strips in a single layer in the air fryer basket. Cut strips in half if needed to fit more.
2. Air fry regular cut bacon at 350°F for 7-9 minutes, or until bacon is browned and reaches desired crispiness. Air fry thick-cut bacon for 10-12 minutes.
3. Transfer bacon to a paper towel-lined plate then serve. If cooking bacon in batches, be sure to discard any oil in the drip pan before repeating the process.

Recipe Notes

The nutrition label is per slice of bacon so you can easily calculate depending on how many slices you eat.

Sirloin Steak With Diane Sauce

Ingredients:

- For the steak:
- 2 x 200g sirloin steak (1.5 cm–2.5 cm thick)
- Black and white peppercorns, to taste
- For the Sauce:
- 100g mushrooms (sliced)
- 15g butter
- 1 small onion (chopped)
- 1 clove garlic (minced)
- 200ml double cream
- 200ml beef stock
- 50ml brandy
- 1–2 tbsp Worcestershire sauce
- 1 tbsp olive oil
- 1 tbsp Dijon mustard
- Salt and pepper, to taste

Directions:

1. For the Steak:
2. Pat the steaks with kitchen paper and press the peppercorns into both sides then cover and refrigerate for 2–3 hours.
3. Plug in and switch on the air fryer at the mains power supply.
4. Set the temperature to 200°C and the time according to the guidelines:
5. Rare Approx. 9–10 mins
6. Medium-rare Approx. 10–12 mins
7. Medium Approx. 12–15 mins
8. Medium-well Approx. 15–18 mins
9. Well done Approx. 18–20 mins
10. Carefully place the steaks into the relevant cooking compartment. Turn halfway through cooking.
11. For the sauce:
12. Heat the oil and butter in a frying pan and cook the onion over a medium heat until soft and brown.
13. Add the Worcestershire sauce, brandy and stock to the pan.
14. Cook rapidly, deglazing the pan and stirring continuously. Add the mushrooms, mustard, garlic and cream and season with salt and pepper, to taste. Set aside to cool.
15. Remove the steaks from the air fryer and leave to rest for approx. 5 mins; slice diagonally into strips.
16. Add the steak to the sauce and stir in the meat juices.
17. Serve immediately with your choice of sides.

Air Fryer Filet Mignon

Servings: 2

Cooking Time: 12 Minutes

Ingredients:

- 2 filet mignon about 4-6 ounces each
- 1 tbsp olive oil
- 1/2 tsp salt
- 1/2 tsp pepper
- OPTIONAL: Blue Cheese Butter, Garlic Herb Butter, or Garlic Butter

Directions:

1. To prepare the filets, pat steaks dry, then coat the steaks with oil on the top and bottom of each piece.
2. Then, season with salt and pepper, according to your preferences.
3. Transfer steaks to the air fryer basket. Air fry at 380 degrees F for 10 to 12 minutes. Flip steaks halfway through cooking.
4. Use meat thermometer to confirm preferred doneness. Once cooked, for extra tender steak, let steak rest for about 5-10 minutes before eating.

Notes

The exact cook time will depend on how well you like your steak and wattage of your air fryer.

We wanted medium steak, so we cooked them for about 6 minutes on each side. Be sure to use a meat thermometer to confirm the internal temperature.

Air Fryer Memphis-style Bbq Pork Ribs

Servings: 2

Ingredients:

- 1 tablespoon kosher salt
- 1 tablespoon dark brown sugar
- 1 tablespoon sweet paprika
- 1 teaspoon garlic powder
- 1 teaspoon onion powder
- 1 teaspoon poultry seasoning
- 1/2 teaspoon mustard powder
- 1/2 teaspoon freshly ground black pepper
- 2 1/4 pounds individually cut St. Louis–style pork spareribs

Directions:

1. In a large bowl, whisk together the salt, brown sugar, paprika, garlic powder, onion powder, poultry seasoning, mustard powder, and pepper. Add the ribs and toss and rub the seasonings into them with your hands until they're fully coated.
2. Arrange the ribs in the air fryer basket standing up on their ends and leaned up against the wall of the basket and each other. Cook at 350°F until the ribs are tender inside and golden brown and crisp on the outside, about 35 minutes. Transfer the ribs to plates and serve hot.

Breaded Pork Cutlets With Lime

Servings: 4

Cooking Time: 15 Minutes

Ingredients:

- 4 5 oz thin sliced lean pork sirloin cutlets
- seasoned salt (such as adobo)
- 2 large egg whites (beaten)
- 1/2 teaspoon sazon (homemade or packaged)
- 1/2 cup seasoned breadcrumbs (or gluten-free crumbs)
- 1 1/2 tbsp olive oil
- lime wedges for serving

Directions:

1. Season cutlets with 3/4 teaspoon seasoned salt.
2. Place bread crumbs in a medium shallow bowl.
3. In another bowl beat egg whites with sazon.
4. Dip pork cutlets in egg whites, then breadcrumb mixture, shaking off excess.
5. Heat a large nonstick frying pan on medium to medium heat. Add the olive oil and pork cutlets, cook about 6 minutes on each side, until golden brown and no longer pink in the center.
6. Serve with lime wedges.
7. Air Fryer Directions:
8. After cutlets are breaded spray both sides with oil and air fry at 400F for 4 minutes on each side, or until golden

Air Fryer Bacon Wrapped Tater Tots

Servings: 4

Cooking Time: 14 Minutes

Ingredients:

- 24 frozen tater tots
- 12 slices bacon
- 1/4 cup brown sugar

Directions:

1. Cut each slice of bacon in half, making 24 bacon slices.
2. Wrap one piece of bacon strip around one tater tot. Seal ends together with toothpicks if necessary.
3. In a medium bowl, toss bacon wrapped tots with brown sugar to coat.

4. Place coated tots in the air fryer basket, without stacking or overlapping.
5. Air fry at 350 degrees F for 14-16 minutes, until bacon reaches your desired crispness, and tater tots are cooked through.

Notes

Optional Favorite Dipping Sauce: Hot onion dip, ranch dressing, honey mustard, blue cheese dressing or sriracha aioli.

Optional Additional Toppings: Honey glaze, green onions or chives, spicy maple glaze, shredded cheese or grated parmesan cheese.

Cooking Tips: Use a silicone baking mat for easy clean up.

Air Fryer Pork Tenderloin Recipe

Servings: 4

Cooking Time: 20 Minutes

Ingredients:

- 1.5 lbs. pork tenderloin
- 1 tablespoon brown sugar
- 1 tablespoon garlic powder
- 2 teaspoons smoked paprika
- 1 teaspoon onion powder
- 1 teaspoon kosher salt
- 1 teaspoon dried thyme
- ½ teaspoon mustard powder
- 1/2 teaspoon pepper
- 2 tablespoons olive oil

Directions:

1. Preheat the air fryer to 400°F. Spray the air fryer basket with non-stick cooking spray.
2. Make the dry rub. Add the brown sugar, garlic powder, paprika, onion powder, salt, thyme, mustard, and pepper into a bowl and mix until well combined.
3. Pat the pork tenderloin with a paper towel to remove excess moisture and then season the pork with the dry rub.
4. Drizzle a tablespoon of olive oil onto the air fryer basket.
5. Place the pork tenderloin in the air fryer basket. Drizzle the pork with the remaining olive oil.
6. Cook the pork for 10 minutes at 400°F, flip the pork, and cook for an additional 10-12 minutes.

7. Check the internal temperature of the pork and when it reaches an internal temperature of 145°F remove it from the air fryer. Cook the pork tenderloin longer if a more well done pork tenderloin is desired.
8. Remove the pork from the air fryer and let it rest for about 5 minutes before slicing.

Notes

Many pork tenderloins come in 2 packs (two, 1.5-lb. tenderloins). If that is the case, you can use one tenderloin for this recipe and freeze the another tenderloin. Or? You can double this recipe and end up with 2 pork tenderloins.

If you prefer a more rare tenderloin, take the pork tenderloin out of the air fryer when it reaches 138-140°F and it will continue to cook while resting and produce a slightly pink, juicy center.

Feel free to use 1-2 tablespoons of your favorite dry rub or of our pork dry rub for a bit of a different flavor.

Bacon Cheddar Cauliflower Tots

Servings: 4

Cooking Time: 45 Minutes

Ingredients:

- 2 pounds cauliflower florets
- 1 ½ teaspoons kosher salt divided
- 8 ounces sharp cheddar cheese shredded (approx 2 cups)
- 12 bacon strips cooked and crumbled
- ¼ cup cornmeal
- 2 eggs
- 1 teaspoon mustard powder
- ½ teaspoon garlic powder
- ½ teaspoon onion powder
- ½ teaspoon cayenne pepper

Directions:

1. Using a grater, grate the florets until they are the size of cooked rice grains. Put the cauliflower into a bowl that is lined with a clean kitchen towel.
2. Sprinkle 1 teaspoon of salt over the cauliflower and let it sit at room temperature for 5 minutes. Fold the towel ends over the top of the bowl and microwave it for 2 minutes.
3. Remove from the microwave and unfold the towel letting it cool down until it is comfortable to handle.

Once cool, gather up the towel ends and twist while squeezing the cooked cauliflower to remove as much moisture as possible.

4. Preheat the oven to 425°F. Line two half-sheet pans with parchment paper.
5. Empty any liquid that remains in the bowl and add the cooked cauliflower into it, add the remaining ingredients and stir vigorously until fully combined.
6. Use a small cookie scoop to portion the mixture and place 1 ½ inches apart on the prepared pan to allow room for spreading. Gently pat the tots to flatten slightly.
7. Bake for 25 minutes or until golden brown on top with a dark brown on the bottom.
8. Let the tots stand for 2 minutes on the pan before serving.

Notes

These can be cooked in an air fryer at 400°F for 12 minutes (flip after 6 minutes).

Be sure to squeeze the cauliflower very dry.

Philly Cheesesteaks

Servings: 4

Cooking Time: 25 Minutes

Ingredients:

- 1½ pounds boneless top sirloin, cut into ⅛-inch-thick strips
- 1½ cups bell peppers, thinly sliced
- ½ yellow onion, thinly sliced
- 1 teaspoon olive oil
- 4 slices provolone cheese
- 4 French-style hoagie rolls, halved and toasted
- Freshly ground black pepper, to taste
- Kosher salt, to taste

Directions:

1. Place the cut sirloin, bell peppers, onions, and olive oil in a medium bowl, season to taste with kosher salt and freshly ground black pepper, and toss to combine.
2. Place the crisper plate into the Smart Air Fryer basket, then place the sirloin and pepper mixture onto the crisper plate.
3. Select the Roast function, adjust temperature to 395°F, then press Start/Pause.

4. Spread the 4 slices of provolone cheese over the cooked sirloin and peppers.
5. Select the Broil function, adjust time to 5 minutes, then press Start/Pause.
6. Remove the cheesesteak filling when done.
7. Build the sliders on the hoagie rolls and serve warm.

Air Fryer Ham Steaks

Servings: 2

Cooking Time: 10 Minutes

Ingredients:

- 1 ham steak (about 1/2 inch thick, 1/2 lb. (1.25 cm - 227g))
- 2 Tablespoons (30 ml) melted butter
- 1 Tablespoon (15 ml) brown sugar
- 1 teaspoon (5 ml) honey
- 1 Tablespoon (15 ml) orange juice, pineapple juice or apple juice
- 1 teaspoon (5 ml) mustard (optional)

Directions:

1. Make the glaze: In bowl mix melted butter, brown sugar, honey, juice, and optional mustard.
2. Cut ham into steaks if needed. Make sure they are a size that will fit in your air fryer. Brush both sides of ham steak with glaze.
3. Place ham steak in a single layer in air fryer basket/rack. Air fry at 380°F/193°C for about 5 minutes.
4. Flip the steaks and brush a little more glaze on top. Air fry for another 2-4 minutes or until the ham is brown and cooked to your liking.
5. Brush with remaining glaze if desired before serving the ham.

Air-fried Mini Italian Meatloaves Stuffed With Cheese

Servings: 4

Ingredients:

- 1 egg, lightly beaten
- ⅓ cup milk
- 1 clove garlic, minced
- 2 tablespoon purchased basil pesto
- ¼ teaspoon black pepper
- 1 pound 90% lean ground beef
- ⅓ cup Italian seasoned fine dry bread crumbs
- 8 slices pepperoni
- 2 ounce fresh mozzarella pearls (such as BelGioioso)
- ½ cup marinara sauce, warmed
- Chopped fresh basil (optional)
- Grated Parmesan (optional)

Directions:

1. In a medium bowl combine first 5 ingredients (through pepper). Add ground beef and bread crumbs. Combine, being careful not to overmix.
2. Divide meat mixture into four portions. Press a well into each portion, leaving 1/2-inch border around the edge. Place 2 slices of pepperoni in each well, shingling to cover the length of the well. Top each with about 6 mozzarella pearls. Press meat mixture around the filling to enclose. Shape each portion into an oblong loaf shape.
3. Place loaves in basket of air fryer, in batches. Cook at 370°F for about 15 minutes or until an instant-read thermometer inserted in the thickest portion of meat reaches 165°F. Serve topped with warm marinara sauce, fresh basil and Parmesan, if desired.

Spicy Cumin Lamb Skewers

Ingredients:

- 1 tbsp red chili flakes
- 1 tbsp cumin seed
- 2 tsp fennel seed
- 1 tsp kosher salt
- 2 tsp granulated garlic
- 1 ¼ lbs. lamb shoulder chops, cut into 1 inch pieces and bones discarded
- 1 tbsp vegetable oil
- 2 tsp pale dry sherry

Directions:

1. In a mortar and pestle grinder, coarsely grind the chili flakes, cumin and fennel. Add the granulated garlic and kosher salt and briefly grind to break into smaller pieces. Thoroughly combine the ingredients together.
2. Reserve 1 tablespoon of the spice mix in a small bowl. In a large bowl, add the lamb slices in and toss thoroughly with the remaining spice mix, oil and wine.
3. Place the seasoned lamb slices onto the skewers and place in the Air Fryer Oven. Using the Rotisserie setting, air fry the skewers at 340°F for 10 minutes.
4. When the skewers are nearly cooked through, sprinkle the reserved spice mix (optional) on them and let them finish cooking.
5. Remove the skewers from the oven and serve immediately.

Air Fryer Stuffed Peppers

Servings: 4

Cooking Time: 12 Minutes

Ingredients:

- 4 bell peppers
- 1 pound of lean ground beef
- 1 cup of cooked rice
- 1 Tablespoon of olive oil
- 2 cups of tomato sauce
- ½ onion, chopped
- ½ Tablespoon minced garlic
- Salt and pepper to taste
- 1 teaspoon of Italian seasoning
- ¾ cup of shredded mozzarella
- Optional: parsley for garnish

Directions:

1. Preheat your air fryer to 300 degrees.
2. Cut the tops of the peppers off and then scrape out the seeds.
3. Cook your rice according to the package directions.
4. Brush your peppers with olive oil, inside and out. Place them into the air fryer basket and cook for 5 minutes.
5. While the peppers are cooking, season your beef with salt and pepper then brown it with the onions and garlic, in a medium saucepan, over medium high heat. Cook till there is no more pink in the beef and then drain the grease.
6. Add the cooked rice, tomato sauce, and Italian seasoning to your beef mixture and simmer for 4 minutes.
7. Scoop the beef mixture into the peppers and place them back into the air fryer. Cook at 350 degrees for 8 minutes. Top them with the shredded mozzarella and place back into the air fryer for another 3-4 minutes, till the tops are golden brown.
8. Remove from the air fryer and enjoy. Top with chopped parsley for additional garnish.

Air Fryer Bacon Wrapped Asparagus

Servings: 4

Cooking Time: 12 Minutes

Ingredients:

- 1 pound asparagus
- 1/2 pound bacon
- 1/2 tablespoon olive oil

Directions:

1. Trim the ends of the asparagus stalks, about one to two inches.
2. Rinse the freshly cut asparagus.
3. Lightly brush the asparagus with olive oil and season as desired.
4. Cut bacon slices in half, then wrap a slice of bacon around two or three stalks of asparagus
5. Place the asparagus in the basket of the air fryer.
6. Cook at 370 degrees Fahrenheit for 12-14 minutes, depending on bacon crispness your prefer.

Notes

If you find larger stalks of asparagus, you can use an entire slice of bacon to wrap them.

Serving size 8 pieces of asparagus, with ½ slice of bacon wrapped around each piece.

KETO: C/4 P/21 F/35

SALADS & SIDE DISHES RECIPES

Air Fryer Artichokes

Servings: 6

Cooking Time: 16 Minutes

Ingredients:

- 3 medium artichokes
- 1 small lemon, juiced (3 tablespoons lemon juice)
- 1 tablespoon olive oil
- Kosher salt, to taste
- Black pepper, to taste

Directions:

1. Preheat your air fryer to 340 degrees F.
2. Rinse the artichokes, then trim the stems and remove the tough outer leaves. Cut them in half lengthwise and remove the fuzzy choke from the inside using a spoon.
3. Pour the lemon juice over the cut sides. Drizzle with olive oil and season with salt and pepper, to taste. Flip them and repeat on the leafy side.
4. Place them cut side down in the air fryer and fry for 12 minutes. Open the air fryer, flip the artichokes, then fry for 4 more minutes.
5. Serve with lemon wedges and your favorite dipping sauce.

Fried Cauliflower

Servings: 4

Cooking Time: 35 Minutes

Ingredients:

- Fried cauliflower
- 2 eggs
- 1/2 cup (110 grams) self-raising flour
- 1/2 cup (125 millilitres) water
- 1/3 cup finely chopped fresh coriander
- vegetable oil, for deep-frying
- 1 small cauliflower, cut into small florets
- 1 cup (280 grams) greek-style yoghurt

Directions:

1. Fried cauliflower
2. In a medium shallow bowl, whisk eggs, flour and the water until batter is smooth. Stir in half the coriander; season.
3. Heat oil in wok. Dip cauliflower in batter; drain off excess. Deep-fry cauliflower, in batches, until browned lightly and tender. Drain on absorbent paper.
4. In a small bowl, combine remaining coriander and yoghurt; season to taste.
5. Serve cauliflower with coriander yoghurt.

Summer Squash And Ricotta Galette

Servings: 6

Ingredients:

- 1 medium zucchini, cut into ¼-inch thick slices
- 1 medium yellow squash, cut into ¼-inch thick slices
- 1 medium Mexican squash, cut into ¼-inch thick slices
- 2 Roma tomatoes, cut into ¼-inch thick slices
- 1 tablespoon kosher salt, plus more to taste
- ¾ cup ricotta cheese, strained
- 3 cloves garlic, minced
- 2 sprigs thyme, finely chopped
- 2 tablespoons parsley, chopped
- ½ cup grated Parmesan cheese, divided
- ½ teaspoon ground black pepper
- 1 lemon, zested
- 1 sheet premade pie crust
- 1 egg, beaten, for egg wash

Directions:

1. Lay the squashes and tomatoes onto a wire rack in a single layer and sprinkle with salt to draw out the moisture.
2. Mix the ricotta cheese, garlic, thyme, parsley, ¼ cup Parmesan cheese, ground black pepper and lemon zest in a small bowl. Season with salt to taste.
3. Place pie crust on top of parchment paper for easy removal after baking.
4. Spread the cheese mixture onto the middle of the pie crust, leaving 2 inches of space around the edges.
5. Place the squashes and tomatoes on top of the cheese mixture, alternating between slices.

6. Fold the edges of the pie crust inward, creating a little blanket around the edges to hold everything in place.
7. Brush the edges of the pie crust with egg wash and sprinkle the top with Parmesan cheese.
8. Place the cooking pot into the base of the Smart Indoor Grill.
9. Select the Bake function, adjust temperature 325°F and time to 20 minutes, then press Start/Pause to preheat.
10. Place the galette into the preheated cooking pot, then close the lid.
11. Remove when done, let cool on a wire rack for 5 minutes, then serve.

Air Fryer Edamame

Servings: 4

Cooking Time: 8 Minutes

Ingredients:
- 2 cups fresh edamame or frozen
- 1 tablespoon olive or avocado oil
- 1/2 teaspoon garlic powder
- 1/2 teaspoon kosher salt

Directions:
1. In a medium bowl, toss edamame in olive oil, garlic powder, and salt until well coated.
2. Transfer edamame to the air fryer basket, without stacking or overlapping.
3. Air fry at 400 degrees F for 8-10 minutes, shaking 2 or 3 times during the cooking process so they get an even cook.
4. Remove the basket from the air fryer and allow them to slightly cool prior to eating. Discard edamame pods and enjoy the seeds.

Notes

Optional Favorite Dipping Sauces: Chili garlic sauce, wasabi and soy sauce, tangy ponzu sauce or siracha or garlic aioli.
Optional Toppings: Toasted sesame seeds, spiced pepitas, a drizzle of reduced balsamic vinegar, sautéed garlic, parmesan cheese, hot sauce or crispy onions.
Substitutions: Sesame oil, refined coconut oil or grapeseed oil.
Cooking Tips: If you are cooking multiple batches place first batches on a baking sheet to evenly cool.

Mother's Luncheon Chicken Salad

Servings: 6

Cooking Time: 14 Minutes

Ingredients:
- 3 thin cut boneless, skinless chicken breasts
- Oil spray, as needed
- ½ tablespoon all-purpose flour (optional)
- 1 teaspoon kosher salt
- ½ teaspoon freshly ground black pepper
- 2 cups green grapes, halved
- 1 green apple, small diced
- 2 celery ribs, small diced
- 1/3 cup plain almonds, roughly chopped
- 2 green onions, finely chopped
- ½ teaspoon freshly ground black pepper
- Herb Dressing
- 3 tablespoons mayonnaise
- 2 tablespoons grapeseed oil
- 2 tablespoons rice wine vinegar
- ½ lemon, juiced
- 1 tablespoon fresh tarragon, finely chopped
- 1 tablespoon fresh chives, finely chopped
- Kosher salt, to taste

Directions:
1. Insert the crisper plate into the Smart Air Fryer basket.
2. Place the chicken breasts in a medium bowl, spray them with oil, then toss them to coat with the salt, pepper, and flour.
3. Place the chicken onto the crisper plate.
4. Select the Chicken function and adjust the time to 14 minutes, then press Start/Pause.
5. Whisk together all of the dressing ingredients in a small bowl, then season to taste with salt.
6. Remove the chicken from the air fryer and let cool to room temperature, then finely dice and toss with the remaining ingredients except the lettuce, and toss enough of the dressing to coat.
7. Serve the chicken mixture on a bed of the lettuce.

Air Fryer Potato Croquettes

Servings: 8

Cooking Time: 15 Minutes

Ingredients:

- 850 g Frozen potato croquette
- Salt to serve optional
- Cooking oil spray

Directions:

1. Preheat the air fryer to 195C/385F for 5 minutes
2. Remove the air fryer basket and spray lightly with cooking oil spray
3. Remove the croquettes from the packaging and arrange them in the air fryer basket in a single layer. Make sure they are not overcrowded but it is ok if they are touching slightly.
4. Cook for 15-18 minutes until crispy and golden brown on the outside flipping the croquettes halfway through the cooking time.
5. Remove the basket from the air fryer, transfer the croquettes to a plate and serve immediately with any dipping sauce of choice.

Notes

How to store leftovers

Leftover potato croquettes can be stored in an airtight container in the fridge for up to 2 days.

To reheat, preheat your air fryer to 160C/365F and cook the croquettes for 5-7 minutes until heated through. Do not overcook as this will make the croquettes dry out. Do not freeze thawed potato croquette.

Air-fryer Crispy Pork Belly With Mandarin Salad

Servings: 6

Cooking Time: 50 Minutes

Ingredients:

- 1kg pork belly
- 2 tsp sea salt flakes
- 1 tbs Dijon mustard
- 1 tbs Woolworths pure honey
- 1 tbs white wine vinegar
- 1 tbs extra virgin olive oil
- 3 mandarins, peeled, cut crossways thickly sliced
- 60g baby rocket leaves
- 1/2 red onion, thinly sliced into rounds
- 1 fennel bulb, trimmed, thinly sliced

Directions:

1. Preheat air fryer to 200°C. Pat pork dry with paper towels. Rub salt flakes into rind. Line air-fryer basket with foil. Place pork belly, skin-side up, in basket and cook for 30 minutes or until skin is crisp. Reduce heat to 160°C and cook for a further 20 minutes or until pork is cooked through. Rest for 15 minutes. Meanwhile, combine mustard, honey, vinegar and oil in a small bowl. Just before serving, toss mandarin, rocket, onion and fennel in a large bowl.
2. Serve sliced pork with salad drizzled with mustard dressing

Air Fryer Hush Puppies

Servings: 16

Cooking Time: 6 Minutes

Ingredients:

- 1 package of Jiffy Mix (8.5 ounce box)
- 1/4 cup all-purpose flour
- 1/4 teaspoon garlic powder
- 1/3 cup whole milk
- 1 egg
- 2 tablespoons onion, diced
- 1-2 tablespoons jalapeno pepper (or sweet pepper), diced
- OPTIONAL
- pinch of cayenne pepper

Directions:

1. Mix together the Jiffy Mix, flour, garlic powder, and cayenne pepper (if using).
2. Add in the milk and egg and mix to combine.
3. Add the diced onions and peppers and mix to just combine.
4. Preheat the air fryer to 350 degrees and let the mix rest for 5 minutes.
5. Lay down parchment paper rounds* and place drops of hush puppy dough using a cookie scoop or spoon.
6. Cook for about 6 minutes, flipping with 1-2 minutes left.
7. Carefully remove from air fryer and serve.
8. Refrigerate for up to 7 days or freeze for up to 3 months.

Notes

*must use parchment paper or foil or the mix will stick to the air fryer basket.

To reheat from refrigerated:

Preheat air fryer to 350 degrees and cook for 3-4 minutes until heated thoroughly.

To reheat from frozen:

Preheat air fryer to 350 degrees and cook for 4-5 minutes until heated thoroughly.

Grilled Salad With Raspberry Poppy Seed Dressing

Ingredients:

- 6-8 small-medium hearts of Romaine
- olive oil
- salt & pepper
- Raspberry Poppy Seed Dressing:
- 1/3 cup confectioners' sugar
- ¼ cup raspberry vinegar
- 2 tbsp orange juice
- ½ tsp onion powder
- ¼ tsp salt
- ¼ tsp ground ginger
- 1/3 cup canola oil
- ½ tsp poppy seeds

Directions:

1. In a blender, combine the first six ingredients for the dressing. While blending, gradually add in canola oil until all of the ingredients are blended smooth. Transfer dressing to a mixing bowl and stir in poppy seeds. Refrigerate until ready to serve.
2. Preheat grill to medium high. Brush all romaine halves with olive oil evenly on both sides. Season with salt and pepper to your liking. Place them on the grill and cook for 2-3 minutes per side, or until nicely charred. Drizzle chilled salad dressing on top and enjoy!

Air Fryer Shishito Peppers

Servings: 4

Cooking Time: 6 Minutes

Ingredients:

- 8 ounces shishito peppers, washed and thoroughly dried
- 2 teaspoons olive oil
- 1 tablespoon lemon juice
- ½ teaspoon coarse salt
- ½ cup mayo
- 1 tablespoon lemon juice
- ½ teaspoon paprika
- ¼ teaspoon garlic powder

Directions:

1. Preheat your air fryer to 390 F.
2. Toss peppers with oil in a large bowl until evenly coated.
3. Place in an even layer in the preheated air fryer basket and cook for 6 minutes, shaking the basket halfway through.
4. While the peppers are roasting, prepare a dipping sauce by mixing together the mayo, lemon juice, paprika, and garlic powder until well combined.
5. Transfer the cooked peppers to a platter, drizzle lemon juice over top, and sprinkle with salt.
6. Enjoy immediately with dipping sauce.

Crispy Brussels Sprouts Salad

Servings: 2

Ingredients:

- 200 g Brussel sprouts
- 1 Shallot, sliced
- 15 g fresh mint
- 15 fresh parsley
- 2 tbsp Pomegranate seeds
- 2 tbsp lemon juice
- 2 tsp olive oil
- 1 tsp hot sauce, optional

Directions:

1. Slice the Brussels in half and larger ones in 3. Then add the sliced Brussels and shallot to the air fryer, for around 10 minutes - giving it a shake half way through.
2. To a bowl add the herbs and combine with the oil and lemon juice. Mix through with the crispy sprouts.
3. Add the pomegranate seeds and the hot sauce - if you're using, serve straight away.

VEGETABLE & & VEGETARIAN RECIPES

Air Fryer Moroccan-spiced Carrots

Cooking Time: 2-4 Minutes

Ingredients:

- 1 lb. medium carrots, peeled, trimmed, and cut ½"-thick on the bias
- 1 tbsp. extra-virgin olive oil
- 1/2 tsp. ground cinnamon
- 1/2 tsp. ground coriander
- 1/2 tsp. ground cumin
- 1/2 tsp. kosher salt
- 1/2 tsp. smoked paprika
- 2 tbsp. fresh orange juice
- 2 tsp. fresh lemon juice
- 1/4 c. pomegranate seeds
- 2 tbsp. chopped toasted almonds
- Torn fresh mint leaves, for serving

Directions:

1. In a medium bowl, toss carrots, oil, cinnamon, coriander, cumin, salt, and paprika. Scrape into an air-fryer basket; reserve bowl. Cook at 370° until carrots are just tender, about 13 minutes.
2. In reserved bowl, combine orange juice and lemon juice. Add hot carrots and toss to coat. Top with pomegranate seeds, almonds, and mint.

Air Fryer Potatoes

Servings: 4

Ingredients:

- 1 lb. baby potatoes, halved
- 1 tbsp. extra-virgin olive oil
- 1 tsp. garlic powder
- 1 tsp. Italian seasoning
- 1 tsp. Cajun seasoning (optional)
- Kosher salt
- Freshly ground black pepper
- Lemon wedge, for serving
- Freshly chopped parsley, for garnish

Directions:

1. In a large bowl, toss potatoes with oil, garlic powder, Italian seasoning, and Cajun seasoning, if using. Season with salt and pepper.
2. Place potatoes in basket of air fryer and cook at 400° for 10 minutes. Shake basket and stir potatoes and cook until potatoes are golden and tender, 8 to 10 minutes more.
3. Squeeze lemon juice over cooked potatoes and garnish with parsley before serving.

Air Fryer Broccoli Recipe

Cooking Time: 5 Minutes

Ingredients:

- 5 cups Broccoli florets
- 3 tbsp Olive oil
- 1/2 tbsp Lemon juice
- 1/2 tsp Garlic powder
- 1/2 tsp Sea salt
- 1/4 tsp Black pepper

Directions:

1. Preheat the air fryer to 380 degrees F (193 degrees C).
2. In a large bowl, drizzle broccoli with olive oil and lemon juice. Season with garlic powder, salt, and pepper. Toss to coat.
3. Arrange the broccoli florets in the air fryer, working in batches if needed, depending on the size of your air fryer basket. Air fry for 5 minutes, until broccoli

is tender and the edges are browned. (Time will vary depending on the size of your florets.)

Gouda And Bacon Stuffed Mushrooms

Servings: 16

Cooking Time: 30 Minutes

Ingredients:

- 1 pound white button mushrooms, thoroughly cleaned
- 8 strips bacon (not thick cut)
- 1/2 yellow onion, diced
- 8 ounces gouda cheese, grated
- 1/2 cup
- bread crumbs
- 1/2 teaspoon dried thyme

Directions:

1. Preheat your oven to 400°F
2. Cut the stems out of the mushrooms:
3. Use a small paring knife to cut the stems out of each mushroom. Make a good-sized divot in the mushrooms, but make sure to leave enough mushroom around the edges to hold the filling. Finely dice the stems and cored bits.
4. Cook the bacon:
5. Meanwhile, add bacon to a medium or large skillet over medium heat. Cook until bacon is browned and crispy, about 6 to 7 minutes. Remove the cooked bacon, leaving the grease, and chop into tiny bits.
6. Cook the filling ingredients:
7. Add the chopped mushroom cores, diced onions, and thyme to the skillet with the reserved bacon grease. Sauté the filling ingredients over medium heat until the onions are soft, about 5 minutes. Remove from heat and stir in breadcrumbs and chopped bacon. Let cool.
8. Add the gouda:
9. After mixture has cooled slightly, stir in the grated gouda cheese.
10. Stuff the mushrooms:
11. Line up the cored mushrooms in a baking dish that has been lightly oiled to prevent sticking. Spoon about 2 heaping tablespoons of the filling into each mushroom, piling it high and packing it in. It's okay if the mushrooms are almost overflowing. You should use all the filling!
12. Bake the mushrooms:
13. Bake the stuffed mushrooms for 20 minutes at 400F. Let cool slightly before serving.
14. Stuffed mushrooms can be made completely in advance and reheated in a 350 F oven until warmed through. They keep fine in the fridge for up to 3 days.

Crispy Garlic & Herb Baby Potatoes

Servings: 4

Cooking Time: 20 Minutes

Ingredients:

- 450g baby potatoes, halved
- 1 tbs olive oil
- 1 tsp garlic powder
- 1 tsp rosemary, fresh, chopped
- 1/2 tsp thyme, dried
- 1 tbs chives, fresh, chopped
- 1 pinch black pepper (to taste)

Directions:

1. Place the potatoes in a large bowl, add the oil, garlic powder, rosemary and thyme and toss well to coat.
2. Heat the air fryer to 200°C and cook the potatoes for 10 minutes, toss well and cook for 10 more minutes until golden and crisp.
3. Season with black pepper, top with chopped chives and serve.

Cauliflower Wings

Servings: 2-4

Cooking Time: 15 Minutes

Ingredients:

- 1 medium head of cauliflower, cut into florets
- 1 cup all purpose flour
- 1 cup soy milk
- 1/2 tsp salt
- 1/2 tsp pepper
- 1/2 tsp garlic powder
- Breadcrumbs or almond flour
- Sauce:
- 1/3 cup smooth peanut butter
- 1 tbsp soy sauce
- 1 tbsp chilli paste (Sriracha or peri peri)
- 1 tsp sesame oil
- 1 tbsp lime juice
- 2 tsp honey or coconut sugar
- 1 small garlic clove, minced
- 1 tsp grated ginger
- 4 tbsp water
- Other:
- Sliced green onion to top
- Sesame seeds to top

Directions:

1. Preheat the Instant Pot Duo Crisp with the air fryer lid and set the temperature to 180 degrees for 12 minutes.
2. Mix the flour, soy milk salt, pepper and garlic powder together in a bowl until smooth
3. Dip each piece of cauliflower into the batter, let any excess batter drip off then place the
4. Cauliflower bites in breadcrumb's, coat well and place on the frying rack of the Instant pot.
5. Place in the Instant pot and air-fry for 10-13 minutes (check so they don't burn) remove and
6. dip in the sauce, place back in the air fryer and air fry for another 3 minutes or so.
7. For the sauce: place all the sauce ingredients together in a small pot until combined and
8. creamy, store the rest of the sauce for extra dipping of other vegetables and chips.
9. Top the cauliflower wings with sliced green onions and sesame seeds.
10. Enjoy!

Air-fryer Brussels Sprouts

Servings: 8

Ingredients:

- 4 slices center-cut bacon
- 2 ½ pounds Brussels sprouts, trimmed and halved lengthwise
- 1 large red onion, roughly chopped
- 1 tablespoon extra-virgin olive oil
- ¾ teaspoon salt
- ¼ teaspoon ground pepper
- 2 tablespoons fresh lemon juice
- 2 teaspoons fresh thyme leaves

Directions:

1. Place bacon in a single layer in the basket of an air fryer. Air-fry at 400 degrees F until the bacon is crisp, about 14 minutes, flipping once halfway through. Transfer to a paper-towel-lined plate.
2. Toss Brussels sprouts, onion, oil, salt and pepper in a large bowl. Place about half of the Brussels sprouts mixture in a single layer in the air fryer basket. Air-fry at 375 degrees F until browned and crispy, 14 to 16 minutes, flipping once halfway through. Transfer to a serving platter. Repeat with the remaining Brussels sprouts mixture. Drizzle with lemon juice; sprinkle with thyme. Crumble the cooked bacon over the top.

Teriyaki Tofu

Servings: 3

Cooking Time: 25 Minutes

Ingredients:

- For The Tofu
- 1 block (250 g) firm tofu drained (see notes)
- 1-1½ Tbsp cornstarch or arrowroot flour
- ½ tsp onion powder
- ½ tsp garlic powder
- ¼ tsp black pepper
- ½ tsp salt
- For The Sauce
- 3-4 Tbsp maple syrup (see notes)
- 2 tsp fresh ginger minced
- 1½ tsp fresh garlic minced
- 2½ Tbsp low sodium soy sauce or tamari or coconut aminos

- ½ cup (120 ml) water
- 2 Tbsp lemon juice or rice vinegar
- 1 Tbsp cornstarch or arrowroot flour + 2 Tbsp water
- 2 Tbsp mirin or dry sherry (optional)
- Other Ingredients:
- Cooked rice or rice noodles
- Pan-fried veggies of choice (e.g. red pepper)
- Cooking spray
- Fresh chives chopped
- Sesame seeds

Directions:

1. You can watch the video in the post for visual instructions.
2. Preheat the oven to 400 °F/200 °C and line a baking sheet with parchment paper.
3. Press the tofu for at least 15 minutes. Then cut it into small, bite-sized cubes (about 1-inch) or triangles.
4. To press the tofu, place the block between two layers of paper towels, then place a cutting board on top and something heavy like a cast-iron skillet or several heavy books.
5. Next, combine the cornstarch, onion powder, garlic powder, black pepper, and salt in a medium bowl (or Ziplock bag), add the tofu, and toss to thoroughly coat the tofu.
6. Transfer the tofu to a parchment-lined baking sheet in a single layer. Spray liberally with cooking oil and bake for about 25 minutes, flipping halfway, until the tofu is golden-brown and crispy.
7. Alternatively, air fry the tofu at 400 °F/200 °C for 12-14 minutes, shaking halfway. At the same time, prepare any sides like veggies, noodles, rice, etc.
8. Meanwhile, prepare the sauce by mincing the garlic and ginger, and combine them with the remaining sauce ingredients in a skillet. Bring to a simmer, stirring often.
9. Combine the cornstarch with two tablespoons of water and stir into a lump-free slurry.
10. Add that to the skillet and increase to medium-high heat, constantly stirring, until the sauce thickens. Then, remove it from the heat. Taste test and adjust any ingredients to your liking. i.e., more maple, soy sauce, etc.
11. Add the tofu to the sauce, toss well, and then serve with your side of choice, garnished with sesame seeds and finely chopped scallions or chives. Enjoy!

Notes

Maple syrup: You can use any other liquid sweetener of choice.

Add veggies of choice: I used peppers because they pair well with this sweet and sour sticky tofu, however, you can use other veggies of choice.

Tofu: If you can't eat tofu because of a soy allergy, I would recommend making my chickpea tofu recipe and adding 1 tsp of agar powder for firmer tofu.

Freeze leftover sauce: You can double the sauce recipe and freeze leftovers. The teriyaki sauce not only tastes great over tofu, but also over roasted veggies!

Air-fryer Cumin Carrots

Servings: 4

Cooking Time: 15 Minutes

Ingredients:

- 2 teaspoons coriander seeds
- 2 teaspoons cumin seeds
- 1 pound carrots, peeled and cut into 41/2-inch sticks
- 1 tablespoon melted coconut oil or butter
- 2 garlic cloves, minced
- 1/4 teaspoon salt
- 1/8 teaspoon pepper
- Minced fresh cilantro, optional

Directions:

1. Preheat air fryer to 325°. In a dry small skillet, toast coriander and cumin seeds over medium heat 45-60 seconds or until aromatic, stirring frequently. Cool slightly. Grind in a spice grinder, or with a mortar and pestle, until finely crushed.
2. Place carrots in a large bowl. Add melted coconut oil, garlic, salt, pepper and crushed spices; toss to coat. Place on greased tray in air-fryer basket.
3. Cook until crisp-tender and lightly browned, 12-15 minutes, stirring occasionally. If desired, sprinkle with cilantro.

Air Fryer Baked Potatoes

Servings: 4

Cooking Time: 50 Minutes

Ingredients:

- 4 potatoes, thoroughly cleaned
- 2 tbs olive oil
- 1 tbs sea salt
- 1 pinch black pepper
- 1 tbs garlic powder
- 1 tbs dried parsley
- 4 tbs butter

Directions:

1. Preheat the air fryer to 200°C.
2. Brush the potatoes with olive oil and season with salt, pepper, garlic powder, and parsley. Arrange the potatoes in the air fryer basket. Cook until soft. Slice the potatoes in the middle lengthwise. Pinch both sides of the potato so that it will open up. Top each potato with butter.

Air Fryer Red Potatoes

Servings: 4

Cooking Time: 12 Minutes

Ingredients:

- 2 pounds baby red potatoes
- 2 Tablespoons olive oil
- 1 teaspoon dried Rosemary
- 1 Tablespoon garlic powder
- 1/2 teaspoon Kosher salt
- 1/2 teaspoon ground black pepper

Directions:

1. Preheat the air fryer to 400 degrees Fahrenheit/200 degrees Celcius.
2. Rinse and clean the potatoes in cold water.
3. Place them on a cutting board and pat dry with paper towels.
4. Next cut potatoes into wedges in equal sized pieces.
5. Transfer potatoes into a large bowl and drizzle potato wedges with olive oil.
6. Sprinkle the potato wedges with crushed rosemary, garlic powder, salt and pepper.
7. Place the seasoned potatoes in a single layer in the air fryer basket.

8. Air fry at 400 degrees F for 10-12 minutes, flipping halfway through the cooking process until the potatoes are golden brown and tender.
9. Serve while hot.

Notes

I make this recipe in my Cosori 5.8 qt. air fryer. Depending on your air fryer, size and wattages cook time may need to be adjusted a couple of minutes.

Optional Toppings: Fresh thyme, grated parmesan cheese, chopped chives or parsley, sour cream, olive tapenade, gooey cheese sauce or cover them with chili and diced onions.

Optional Favorite Dipping Sauces: Tzatziki sauce, ranch dressing, spicy ketchup, horseradish aioli, nutty tahini dip, barbecue sauce, tangy cucumber-yogurt sauce or honey Dijon sauce.

Substitutions: If you are out of olive oil, you can use avocado oil, refined coconut oil, sunflower oil or canola oil in its place.

Air Fryer Kung Pao Brussels Sprouts

Servings: 2-4

Ingredients:

- Brussels Sprouts:
- Combine the following in a large bowl:
- 4 cups brussels sprouts, outer layer peeled and quartered
- 2 tbsp extra virgin olive oil like Lucini Italia Premium Select
- 1 tsp garlic powder
- pinch of salt and pepper
- 1/4 cup roasted salted peanuts
- Kung Pao Sauce:
- In a small bowl combine the following:
- 3 tbsp soy sauce
- 1 tbsp honey
- 1 tbsp Sriracha
- 1/2 tsp ginger, grated
- 1/2 tsp garlic, grated
- 1/2 tsp rice wine vinegar
- 1/2 tsp crushed red chili flakes

Directions:
1. Preheat the air fryer to 360 degrees.
2. Mix everything listed under brussels sprouts together except for the peanuts and put in the air fryer for 8 minutes, stopping when there are two minutes left- add in the peanuts and continue to cook for the remaining two minutes. If you like your brussels sprouts crispier, cook for an additional few minutes being careful to not burn them.
3. Once the brussels sprouts are done cooking, remove from the air fryer into the same bowl you mixed them in-toss them with the Kung Pao sauce and enjoy immediately!

Lemon Parmesan Air Fryer Asparagus

Servings: 4

Cooking Time: 2 Minutes

Ingredients:
- 1 bunch asparagus see note 1
- 1 tablespoon olive oil
- 1/8 teaspoon salt
- 1/2 lemon to squeeze over
- 1/2 cup parmesan cheese to sprinkle

Directions:
1. Snap or trim the woody ends off the asparagus spears. This is typically the bottom 2 inches.
2. Toss the asparagus in olive oil. Optional but helpful- use your hands to massage it in.
3. Heat the air fryer to 400°F. Cook asparagus for 2-5 minutes, shaking and flipping halfway through.
4. Heat the air fryer to 400°F. Cook asparagus for 2-5 minutes, shaking and flipping halfway through.

Notes

1- asparagus can vary greatly in width, and you may need to adjust the cook time accordingly. Thin asparagus cooked through in 2 minutes, whereas extremely thick asparagus took 5 minutes. Use your best judgement and remove when asparagus is bright green, but before it gets wrinkly.

Storage

Best served fresh, but you can store and reheat:

Cool completely, then store in an air tight container in the fridge for up to 2 days*.

*they are safe to eat but get bitter as they store

Reheating

To reheat, set your air fryer to 350°F. Heat for 3 or so minutes, turning asparagus as needed, until warmed through.

Air Fryer "roasted" Cauliflower

Servings: 6

Cooking Time: 15 Minutes

Ingredients:
- 1 pound cauliflower
- 1/3 cup olive oil
- 3 Tablespoons grated parmesan cheese
- 1/2 teaspoon paprika
- 1/2 teaspoon garlic powder
- 1/4 teaspoon crushed red pepper optional
- salt and pepper to taste

Directions:
1. Start by cutting the cauliflower into small pieces.
2. In a small bowl whisk together olive oil, parmesan, paprika, garlic, crushed red pepper and salt and pepper.
3. Toss the cauliflower with the mixture to coat.
4. Place in air fryer basket at 390 degrees for 13-15 minutes or until crispy.

Air Fryer Blooming Onion

Servings: 4

Cooking Time: 18 Minutes

Ingredients:
- 1 large onion sweet or yellow
- 1 cup all purpose flour
- 1 tablespoon paprika
- 1 teaspoon Italian Seasoning
- 1 tespoon kosher salt
- 1 teapoon garlic powder
- 1 teaspoon chili powder for spicier kick, use cayenne pepper
- 1 cup water
- 1 cup Italian seasoned breadcrumbs

Directions:
1. Because the onion will be very hot, to easily remove the hot onion from the air fryer basket, use a piece of aluminum foil to make an aluminum foil sling for easy lifting.

2. Remove the outer skin of the onion and cut off the top, placing the cut side facing down.

3. Using a cutting board and a sharp knife, slice from the middle of the onion, leaving a small uncut circle in the center. Make 8-10 evenly spaced slices from top to bottom of the entire onion, and through all of the layers, leaving the center connected and root intact to the onion petals.

4. Place onion in ice cold water and let it sit for about 1-2 hours to soften the onion petals to help them separate to coat.

5. In a medium bowl, combine the flour with the spices. Add one cup of water to the dry ingredients, stirring until it forms into a batter. Add one tablespoon of water or extra flour if necessary.

6. Drain onion from the water, patting dry with a paper towel if needed. Open the onion slices, spreading them as much as possible without tearing the center.

7. Place onion in a deep bowl, and dip onion or spoon the batter over the onion, making sure to coat onion sections evenly. Shake of excess batter, and then coat the onion with breadcrumbs.

8. Spray your Air Fryer basket with non-stick cooking spray or line the basket with parchment paper. Place the coated onion cut-side down, in Air Fryer basket.

9. To help your blooming onion crisp, lightly spritz the onion petals with cooking oil spray, and air fry at 380°F for 18-20 minutes until golden brown color with a crispy coating.

Small Jacket Potatoes With Rosemary

Servings: 4

Cooking Time: 24 Minutes

Ingredients:
- 500 g small new potatoes, unpeeled
- ½ tablespoon olive oil
- 1 tablespoon fresh rosemary
- 2 cloves garlic, sliced
- Coarse sea salt
- Freshly ground black pepper

Directions:
1. Preheat the airfryer to 180°C. Scrub the small new potatoes clean under running water and pat them thoroughly dry with kitchen paper.

2. In a bowl coat the small new potatoes with olive oil, rosemary and garlic and transfer them to the fryer basket.

3. Slide the basket into the airfryer and set the timer to 24 minutes to fry the small potatoes crispy and done. Place the fried small potatoes in a serving dish and sprinkle with salt and pepper.

4. Serve the potatoes with grilled meat or fish.

5. Tip: Slice the potatoes into blocks and soak them in water for at least 30 minutes. Drain them thoroughly and then pat them dry with kitchen paper.

How To Make Tomato Soup At Home

Ingredients:
- 2 tbsp olive oil
- 400g tomatoes (quartered)
- 500ml vegetable stock
- 1 tsp sugar
- 2 tsp tomato purée
- 1 medium onion (peeled and diced)
- Salt and pepper, to taste
- If you feel like putting a twist on your recipe, simply add some of these extra ingredients:
- Add leek and peas for a tasty tomato and vegetable soup. For more vegetable soup ideas, have a look at these seasonal variations.

- Throw in a peeled and chopped carrot for a wholesome tomato and carrot soup variation.
- Peel and mince a clove of garlic and some fresh basil for a classic tomato and basil soup recipe that's perfect with some parmesan and croutons.

Directions:

1. Having warmed the olive oil in a large pan, add the onion and cook on a low heat until soft. This will take anywhere from 5 to 10 minutes.
2. Stir in the tomato purée until all of the onion is coated.
3. Now add the tomatoes and sprinkle in some salt and pepper.
4. Stew the mixture for around 10 minutes, releasing all the tomato juices.
5. Gently pour in the stock, stirring as you go.
6. Reduce the heat and cook for around 25 minutes, with the lid on the pan.
7. Finally, transfer your mixture into a blender.

Chickpea Nuggets

Servings: 16

Cooking Time: 18 Minutes

Ingredients:

- Nuggets:
- 8 oz (225 g) broccoli florets
- 1 (15 oz) can of chickpeas (save the liquid!)
- 1/2 onion chopped (I used red)
- 2 cloves of garlic minced
- 1/2 tsp salt
- Black pepper to taste
- 2 tsp nutritional yeast
- 1/4 tsp smoked paprika
- 1/2 cup (45 g) oat flour (gluten-free if needed)
- Breading:
- 3/4 cup breadcrumbs gluten-free, if needed (see notes)
- Cooking spray

Directions:

1. You can watch the short video for visual instructions.
2. Drain the liquid of the chickpea can into a medium bowl and set it aside.
3. Cook the broccoli florets in boiling salted water for about 4 minutes, then drain the water very well.

4. Add the broccoli to a food processor, along with the chickpeas, onion, garlic, and spices.
5. Pulse about 8 times, then add the oat flour. Pulse a couple of more times (making sure not to over-process the mixture), until it's combined, scraping down the sides of the food processor, if needed.
6. Using your hands, shape the mixture into 16 nuggets.
7. Dip each nugget into the chickpea water and then into the breadcrumbs to coat the nuggets from all sides. You can also use your favorite breading. I used this homemade breading.
8. Spray the air fryer basket (or a lined baking sheet) with a little cooking spray and also the nuggets, so that they don't stick and become a little crispier.
9. Air fryer method: Air fry for 18 minutes at 380 F (190 C), flipping after about 12 minutes.
10. Oven method: Bake them in your preheated oven for about 25 minutes at 400 F (205 C) flipping after 15 minutes.
11. Enjoy with this yum yum sauce or a dip of choice.

Notes

If you don't want to use breadcrumbs, then follow this recipe for my homemade breading.

More tips, FAQs, and storing instructions can be found in the blog post above.

Honey Chipotle Roasted Brussels Sprouts

Servings: 4

Cooking Time: 25 Minutes

Ingredients:

- 1 pound Brussels sprouts
- 2 tablespoons olive oil
- 1/4 teaspoon salt
- 1/4 teaspoon black pepper
- 2 chipotle peppers, from a can of chipotles in adobo
- 1/4 cup honey
- 1 tablespoon adobo sauce, from chipotle can

Directions:

1. Preheat oven to 400°F
2. Prepare the sprouts:
3. Cut Brussels sprouts in half through the end and toss with olive oil, salt, and pepper. Spread out

sprouts on an even layer on a baking sheet. Roast for 15 minutes.

4. Prepare the honey-chipotle sauce:
5. Using a small knife, split chipotle peppers in half and remove seeds. Then mince the peppers and add to a small bowl with honey and one tablespoon of adobo sauce from the can.
6. Finish the sprouts:
7. Remove the sprouts from the oven and stir to ensure even cooking, then spread them again into an even single layer on the baking sheet. Toss with the honey chipotle mixture, but reserve a few tablespoons for finishing the sprouts. Return to oven and bake for another 10 minutes.
8. Serve!
9. Drizzle with the remaining few tablespoons of sauce, and serve sprouts while warm.

Vortex Air Fryer Mushroom Stuffed Bell Peppers

Servings: 3

Cooking Time: 17 Minutes

Ingredients:

- 3 large bell peppers
- 1 cup mushrooms sliced
- 1 cup spinach
- 1 cup mozzarella shredded
- 3 eggs

Directions:

1. Preheat the air fryer to 350°F.
2. Cut ¼-inch off the top of the bell pepper and scoop out the seeds.
3. Add the mushrooms and spinach to an air fryer safe pan and cook them until they are tender about 5-6 minutes.
4. Fill the peppers with the mushrooms and spinach, and crack 1 egg into each pepper.
5. Place the peppers in the air-fryer basket and cook for 13-15 minutes or until the egg is cooked. Season with salt & pepper.
6. Sprinkle the mozzarella cheese on top and cook for an additional 2 minutes or until the cheese is melted.

Spicy Sriracha Tofu Rice Bowls

Servings: 2

Cooking Time: 15 Minutes

Ingredients:

- 14 oz extra firm tofu (drained)
- 1 tablespoon plus 2 teaspoons gluten-free Tamari ((or soy sauce) divided)
- 4 teaspoons sriracha (divided)
- 1 tablespoon sesame oil (divided)
- 1 medium scallion (chopped, white and green parts separated)
- 2 teaspoons Thai sweet chili sauce
- For Serving:
- 1 cups cooked brown rice
- 1/2 cup warmed shelled edamame
- 1/2 teaspoon multi color sesame seeds

Directions:

1. Place tofu block between some paper towels and press to absorb extra water.
2. Repeat until tofu feels dry and no more water comes out. Slice across in half lengthwise and then into cubes.
3. In a large bowl stir together 1 tablespoon of the tamari, 2 teaspoons of the sriracha, 2 teaspoons of the sesame and the scallion whites, add the tofu and let sit 10 minutes.
4. Air Fryer Directions:
5. Spray the air fryer basket with oil.
6. Transfer the tofu to the air fryer in a single layer and air fry 370F about 10 to 12 minutes, shaking the basket halfway until slightly golden and crisp on the outside and tender on the inside.
7. Oven Directions:
8. Bake in a preheat oven 400F about 25 minutes, turning halfway.
9. To Finish (air fryer or oven):
10. While it cooks, add the remaining 2 teaspoons sriracha, 2 teaspoons Tamari, 1 teaspoon sesame oil and sweet chili sauce to the bowl.
11. When the tofu is ready, toss it with the sauce to coat until evenly covered. Serve immediately over rice with edamame, sesame seeds and scallion greens.

Notes

Variations:

Swap the tofu with chicken or shrimp.

If you don't have an air fryer, bake the tofu in the oven at 400 degrees for 25 minutes.

Sub coconut aminos or soy sauce for tamari.

Use plain white sesame seeds or omit them if you can't find multi-colored.

Here, I served these crispy tofu bowls with brown rice and edamame for more protein, but cauliflower rice or stir-fried veggies would also be great.

Ninja Foodi Baked Potato

Servings: 4

Cooking Time: 45 Minutes

Ingredients:

- 4 Russet potatoes
- 1 1/2 tablespoons olive oil
- 1 1/2 tablespoons sea salt

Directions:

1. Preheat your Ninja Foodi to 400 degrees on "Air Fry."
2. Poke each potato, then rub them with olive oil and sea salt all around the outside.
3. Place the baked potatoes in the air fryer basket and cook for about 45 minutes until easily pierced with a fork. Medium and large potatoes could take 50-60 minutes.
4. Remove the baked potatoes from the Ninja Foodi, split them in half, and top them with desired toppings!

Notes

HOW TO REHEAT A BAKED POTATO IN THE NINJA FOODI AIR FRYER:

Preheat your Ninja Foodi to 400 degrees.

Place the already cooked baked potatoes in the air fryer and cook for 5 to 6 minutes until heated thoroughly.

Air Fryer Vegetables With Sausage And Ravioli

Servings: 4

Cooking Time: 13 Minutes

Ingredients:

- 12 ounces fresh ravioli
- 6 ounces sausage sliced
- 1 red onion large dice
- 2 peppers large dice
- 1 small zucchini sliced
- Dressing
- 2 tablespoons olive oil
- 1 ½ tablespoons balsamic vinegar
- 1 teaspoon Italian seasoning

Directions:

1. Preheat air fryer to 400°F.
2. Soak the ravioli in hot water in a large bowl for 6 minutes.
3. Toss the vegetables and sausage in a bowl with the dressing and air fry for 6-7 minutes.
4. Strain the ravioli and season with salt and pepper. Add to the air fryer basket with the vegetables and air fry for 5-6 minutes.
5. Cook until vegetables and pasta are tender.

Air Fryer Mushrooms

Servings: 4

Cooking Time: 7 Minutes

Ingredients:

- 16 ounces button mushrooms halved
- 1 clove garlic minced
- 1 tablespoon olive oil
- 1 1/2 tablespoons butter
- 1 tablespoon soy sauce
- 1/2 teaspoon salt
- 1/2 teaspoon pepper
- 1/2 teaspoon garlic powder

Directions:

1. Preheat the air fryer to 180C/350F. Grease an air fryer basket.
2. In a mixing bowl, add all the ingredients and mix well.
3. Transfer the mushrooms to the air fryer basket and cook for 7-8 minutes, shaking halfway through.
4. Remove the mushrooms from the air fryer and sprinkle with fresh parsley.

Notes

TO STORE: Despite their delicate nature, they can still be stored in your fridge for up to 24 hours by placing them in airtight containers.

TO FREEZE: Place the cooked and cooled mushrooms in a shallow container and store them in the freezer for up to one month.

TO REHEAT: Either microwave them for 20-30 seconds or reheat them back up in the air fryer.

Air Fryer Okra

Servings: 4

Cooking Time: 7 Minutes

Ingredients:

- 12 ounces okra, cut into 1/2-inch slices and tops and bottoms removed
- 1/2 cup flour
- 2 eggs
- 1/3 cup cornmeal
- 1/3 cup breadcrumbs
- 1/2 teaspoon paprika
- sea salt or table salt, to taste
- OPTIONAL
- Pinch of cayenne pepper

Directions:

1. Preheat your air fryer to 380 degrees.
2. Set out 2 medium bowls and 1 small bowl. Fill a medium bowl with flour, the small bowl with the eggs, and the remaining medium bowl with the cornmeal, breadcrumbs, paprika, and cayenne pepper (if using).
3. Take turns dipping each piece of okra into the flour mixture, then the eggs, then the cornmeal mixture coating it on all sides each time. I use a fork to bread them faster.
4. Place the breaded okra in the air fryer and spritz them with a little oil, then cook for 7 to 8 minutes until golden brown on the outside.
5. Remove the okra from the air fryer enjoy!

Notes

HOW TO COOK FROZEN BREADED OKRA IN THE AIR FRYER

Preheat your air fryer to 400 degrees.

Place the frozen okra in the air fryer and cook for about 14 minutes, shaking the basket halfway through.

Remove the cooked okra from the air fryer and enjoy!

HOW TO REHEAT OKRA IN THE AIR FRYER

Preheat your air fryer to 350 degrees.

Place the leftover fried okra in the air fryer and cook for about 2 to 3 minutes, until warmed thoroughly.

Remove the okra from the air fryer and enjoy!

FAVORITE AIR FRYER RECIPES

Mozzarella Sticks With Tomato Dip

Servings: 8

Ingredients:
- 8 string cheese sticks
- 2 eggs
- 3 tbsp Plain Flour
- 60g Panko breadcrumbs
- 1 tsp Smoked Paprika
- For the dip:
- 1 Tin chopped tomatoes
- 2 cloves garlic
- 2 tsp dried oregano
- 1 tsp chilli flakes
- 2 tbsp olive oil

Directions:
1. Place the cheese sticks in the freezer for 20 minutes beforehand.
2. Put the flour, eggs and panko breadcrumbs in 3 separate shallow bowls. Generously season the flour with salt and pepper and mix the smoked paprika through the panko breadcrumbs.
3. Dip the cheese sticks first in the flour, then the egg, then the breadcrumbs.Then again into the egg and breadcrumbs for a double coating.
4. Arrange the breaded cheese in one layer in the air fryer and cook for 4 mins at 190c.
5. For the tomato sauce, put all the ingredients in a food processor and blitz till smooth, add the sauce to a small saucepan and cook on a medium heat for 10 mins, serve warm with the cheese sticks.

Air Fryer Hot Pockets

Servings: 2

Cooking Time: 11 Minutes

Ingredients:
- 2 frozen Hot Pockets (any variety)

Directions:
1. Preheat your air fryer to 350 degrees.
2. Place Hot Pockets inside the air fryer without the crisper sleeve and cook for 11-13 minutes, until heated thoroughly.
3. Carefully remove them from the air fryer and place the Hot Pocket crispers back on and let cool.
4. Enjoy! Be careful as the first bite may still be hot.

Notes

How to Heat Up a Hot Pocket Faster

Preheat air fryer to 400 degrees.

Microwave the Hot Pocket for 60 seconds in the crisper sleeve.

3.Carefully remove the Hot Pocket from the microwave and remove from the crisper sleeve.

Heat the Hot Pocket in the air fryer for 3-4 minutes until warmed thoroughly. Then let cool for at least 5 minutes. The Hot Pocket may still be hot upon the first bite.

Air Fryer Spam

Servings: 4

Cooking Time: 10 Minutes

Ingredients:
- 4 pieces Spam

Directions:
1. Preheat your air fryer to 400 degrees F.
2. Use a cutting board to cut spam into slices.
3. Place spam in a single layer into the air fryer basket without overcrowding.
4. Cook the spam for 10-12 minutes at 400 degrees F, flip spam slices halfway through the cooking time.
5. Remove and place spam on a paper towel-lined plate to absorb any excess grease.
6. Serve while hot.

Notes

Optional Favorite Dipping Sauce: Chimichurri sauce, hot sauce, ranch dressing, Dijon mustard, blue cheese, spicy garlic siracha, cilantro yogurt or marinara sauce.

Kitchen Tips: Spray spam with olive oil spray or light spray if you are going to add any spices prior to cooking (this will help the spices adhere to the meat). Try to keep temperature stable the entire time to ensure spam is fully cooked and crispy.

I make this recipe in my Cosori 5.8 qt. air fryer. Depending on your air fryer, size and wattages your cook time may need to be for an additional couple of minutes.

Air Fryer Frozen Mozzarella Sticks

Servings: 4

Cooking Time: 6 Minutes

Ingredients:

- 12 mozzarella sticks frozen
- tomato sauce or ranch for dipping

Directions:

1. Preheat air fryer to 390°F.
2. Place mozzarella sticks in a single layer in the air fryer basket.
3. Cook for 4-6 minutes or just until the cheese starts to leak out. Rest 2 minutes before serving.

Slow Cooker - Green Chile Queso Dip Recipe W Jalapeño

Servings: 8

Cooking Time: 2 Hours

Ingredients:

- FOR THE QUESO DIP:
- 16 oz. (453g) Velveeta Cheese , cut into 1" cubes for quick melting
- 15 oz. (425g) canned chili (no beans)
- 4 oz. (113g) canned diced green chiles
- 1 fresh jalapeno pepper , minced (optional)
- 1/2 teaspoon kosher salt , or to taste
- 1 teaspoon ground cumin
- 2 teaspoons smoked paprika
- 2 teaspoons chili powder
- 1 teaspoon ground chipotle powder
- 1/2 teaspoon ground cayenne pepper

- 1 cup (240ml) Half & Half
- OPTIONS FOR SERVING:
- tortilla chips (preferred!)
- Potato Chips
- Crackers
- Veggies

Directions:

1. In slow cooker, add all the ingredients and stir together well: Velveeta cheese, chili, diced green chiles, fresh jalapeño, sea salt, ground cumin, smoked paprika, chili powder, chipotle powder, ground cayenne pepper and Half and Half.
2. Cook on low for about 3 hours or High for about 2 hours. Stir occasionally to make sure all the cheese melts.
3. Note on slow cookers: Cooking time will vary depending on the size of slow cooker you are using. If you are using larger slow cookers, more of the dip will be spread across the slow cooker so the cheese will melt faster. Smaller slow cookers will take longer to melt and cook the dip. Check the dip each hour, stir and you determine when it's ready to serve.
4. Serve the yummy queso dip with tortilla chips or the other options.

Air Fryer Bbq Little Smokies

Servings: 5

Cooking Time: 10 Minutes

Ingredients:

- 12 oz Lit'l Smokies
- 1/4 cup BBQ sauce
- 2 tbsp brown sugar

Directions:

1. Add the Lit'l Smokies to the prepared air fryer basket and cook at 350 degrees Fahrenheit for 6 minutes. Toss halfway through.
2. Brush the Lit'l smokies with BBQ sauce and then sprinkle the brown sugar over the top. Cook for an additional 2-3 minutes.
3. Carefully remove the sausages from the air fryer and serve.

Notes

All air fryers can cook differently according to the power output, or wattage. I find that cooking them at 350 degrees Fahrenheit for 8-10 minutes is perfect.

Air Fryer Sausage Links

Servings: 4

Cooking Time: 13 Minutes

Ingredients:

- 1 pound sausage links

Directions:

1. Preheat the air fryer to 370 degrees Fahrenheit .
2. Remove sausage links from packaging and break apart.
3. Place the links in the air fryer basket, without stacking.
4. Cook at 370 degrees F for 12-15 minutes, depending on preferred crispness.

Notes

If you are cooking thawed sausage links in your air fryer, shorten the cooking time by about five minutes.

Flaky Caprese Pinwheels

Servings: 8

Ingredients:

- 3 tablespoons of tomato sauce
- 1 sheet puff pastry, thawed
- 2 tablespoons basil pesto
- 1½ cups mozzarella, shredded
- ½ teaspoon ground black pepper
- Items Needed
- Parchment paper

Directions:

1. Spread the tomato sauce onto the top half of the puff pastry and basil pesto onto the bottom, leaving a ¼ inch of the edge bare.
2. Spread the mozzarella on top of the tomato sauce on the puff pastry.
3. Roll the puff pastry tightly starting from the top toward yourself until you get to the bottom.
4. Halve the roll, then cut the halves into quarters. You should end up with 8 pinwheels.
5. Select the Preheat function on the Air Fryer, adjust temperature to 370°F, then press Start/Pause.
6. Line the air fryer basket with parchment paper.

7. Place the pin wheels into the preheated air fryer, leaving ½-inch spaces between each pinwheel.
8. Sprinkle the ground black pepper on top of the wheels.
9. Set temperature to 370°F and time to 15 minutes, then press Start/Pause.
10. Remove the pinwheels when done, then serve.

Air Fryer Dino Nuggets

Servings: 4

Cooking Time: 9 Minutes

Ingredients:

- 16 Chicken nuggets dinosaur shaped, frozen

Directions:

1. Place the dinosaur nuggets into a single layer in the prepared air fryer basket.
2. Air fry dino nuggets at 400 degrees Fahrenheit/200 degrees Celcius for 8-10 minutes.
3. Flip the frozen nuggets halfway through the cooking process. Add an extra minute for extra crispy nuggets.
4. Serve with your favorite dipping sauce.

Notes

I love to serve these yummy dino buddies with carrots and celery. If your little ones aren't a fan of those veggies, you can also serve them with french fries or even sweet potato fries.

Serve these chicken nuggets with fry sauce, ketchup, bbq sauce, honey mustard sauce, Ranch dipping sauce, or buffalo sauce if you like a little spice.

I make this recipe in my Cosori 5.8 qt. air fryer or 6.8 quart air fryer. Depending on your air fryer, size and wattage, cooking time may need to be adjusted 1-2 minutes.

Eggplant Pizza Recipe

Servings: 12

Cooking Time: 22 Minutes

Ingredients:

- 1 large eggplant
- 1 1/2 tbsp olive oil
- 1/2 cup (120 g) tomato sauce (e.g. marinara or pizza sauce)
- 2 garlic cloves minced
- Salt and pepper to taste
- 1 tsp dried oregano
- 3/4 cup (90 g) vegan mozzarella (I used homemade)
- 1/2 cup (90 g) cherry tomatoes halved
- 1/4 cup (45 g) olives sliced
- Fresh basil chopped for garnish

Directions:

1. You can watch the short video for visual instructions.
2. Preheat the oven to 425 °F (220 °C) and line a baking sheet with parchment paper.
3. Slice the eggplant horizontally into ½-inch (1 cm) thick slices. Brush a little olive oil on each side of the slices and place them on the lined baking sheet.
4. Sprinkle with a little salt, pepper, and the half amount of dried oregano. Bake in the oven for 15 minutes.
5. Mix the tomato sauce with the minced garlic, salt, pepper, and the remaining oregano.
6. After 15 minutes, remove the eggplant slices from the oven, and top them with the tomato sauce, vegan mozzarella, and any toppings you like (I used cherry tomatoes and olives).
7. Bake for a further 10-12 minutes. Garnish with fresh basil and enjoy!

Notes

Slice them evenly: So the eggplant pizzas all cook at an even rate.

Don't underbake the eggplant: Eggplant can be spongy and rubbery when not cooked enough.

Don't skip the pre-roast: The first 15 minutes of roasting time are needed to bring out some water from the eggplant slices and get it to the correct texture.

Don't use too many toppings: Otherwise, the eggplant pizza might turn out soggy.

Read the blog post for more tips, FAQs, and serving suggestions.

Air Fryer Cajun Sweet Potato Wedges

Servings: 4

Cooking Time: 25 Minutes

Ingredients:

- 2 teaspoon ground cumin
- 1 teaspoon ground coriander
- 1 teaspoon garlic salt
- ½ teaspoon smoked paprika
- ½ teaspoon dried thyme
- ½ teaspoon dried oregano
- ½ teaspoon cayenne pepper
- 1 kg small sweet potatoes
- 1 tbsp extra virgin olive oil
- to serve: sea salt flakes, chopped coriander (cilantro) and sour cream

Directions:

1. Preheat a 7-litre air fryer to 200°C/400°F for 3 minutes.
2. To make cajun spice mixture, combine cumin, coriander, garlic salt, paprika, thyme, oregano and cayenne pepper in a small bowl.
3. 3Scrub sweet potatoes and pat dry; cut into long thin wedges. Place in a large bowl with oil and the cajun spice mixture; toss well to coat.
4. Taking care, place wedges in the air fryer basket; at 200°C/400°F, cook for 15 minutes, turning halfway through cooking time, or until golden and cocked through.
5. Sprinkle wedges with salt flakes and chopped coriander; serve with sour cream.

Creamy Mac And Cheese

Ingredients:

- 250g boiled paste until al dente
- For the sauce:
- 5 tsp flour
- 60g butter
- 1 clove chopped garlic
- 1 tsp crushed green chilli
- Salt and pepper to taste
- 1/2 tsp onion powder
- 1/2 tsp mustard powder
- 1/2 tsp chilli flakes
- 2 cups milk
- 1 cup fresh cream
- 2 cups mozzarella
- 1 cup gouda or cheddar(your preference)for the top

Directions:

1. Make a roux with your butter and flour. Allow to cook so that you don't get a flour taste. Mix so that it doesn't burn. Cook for roughly 3 minutes.
2. Add milk and cream whisking continuously,you want to keep whisking so your sauce is lump free. Add in garlic, green chilli and other spices. Add in 1 cup mozzarella and whisk until cheese melts. Check seasoning and adjust accordingly.
3. Add your pasta to a dish that will fit in the air fryer, pour in half the sauce, mix and coat well. Add in the remaining cup of mozzarella and mix through. Pour over the remaining sauce and mix well. Top with cheddar/Gouda cheese.
4. Bake in your instantpot vortex air fryer on 160 degrees celsius for 10 minutes until cheese is melted.
5. Serve immediately. Garnish with chopped parsley

2 Ingredient Air Fryer Pizza

Servings: 2

Cooking Time: 10 Minutes

Ingredients:

- 240g (1 cup) natural or Greek yoghurt
- 350g (2 cups) self-raising flour
- grated cheese (enough to sprinkle on 2 small pizzas)
- pizza sauce/passata
- toppings of your choice (pepperoni, pineapple, peppers, chicken etc)

Directions:

1. Mix the self raising flour and yoghurt together (add more flour if necessary) until a dough consistency has been formed.
2. Split dough in
3. Roll each one out on a floured surface.
4. Place on a bit of parchment paper in air fryer basket and cook at 200C/400F for 8 to 10 minutes, turning over half way.
5. Take pizza out and add pizza sauce, grated cheese & any other toppings of your choice.
6. Return to air fryer basket and cook for a further 3 minutes.
7. Repeat with 2nd pizza.

Air Fryer Fried Cheese Sticks

Servings: 6

Cooking Time: 20 Minutes

Ingredients:

- 12 part-skim mozzarella cheese sticks
- ¼ cup cornstarch
- 2 large eggs
- 2 cups italian seasoned breadcrumbs
- ¼ cup grated Parmesan cheese
- oil, for spraying
- marinara sauce, for dipping

Directions:

1. Separate mozzarella cheese sticks and freeze for 2 hours.
2. Place cornstarch in a large plastic bag. In a medium bowl, beat eggs. In a shallow dish or pie pan, combine breadcrumbs and Parmesan cheese. Place frozen cheese sticks in bag with cornstarch and shake. Remove one cheese stick and dip in beaten

egg, shaking off any excess. Press into breadcrumb mixture and place on baking sheet lined with parchment paper. Repeat with remaining cheese sticks. Spray cheese sticks well with oil.

3. Working in batches of 6, place cheese sticks in air fryer basket. Do not overcrowd. Set temperature to 400 degrees. Air fry for 7 minutes, shaking basket frequently during cooking. Turn cheese sticks, and air fry for 3 minutes more. Repeat with remaining cheese sticks. Serve with warm marinara sauce on the side.

Air Fryer Tostones With Cilantro Dip

Servings: 4

Ingredients:

- TOSTONES
- 3 green plantains
- 2 tbsp. lime juice
- Kosher salt
- 3 tbsp. canola oil, divided
- 1/4 tsp. smoked paprika
- DIP
- 1 1/2 c. cilantro
- 1/2 ripe Hass avocado
- 1/2 serrano chile, chopped
- 1 clove garlic
- 1 scallion (green part only), roughly chopped
- 2 tbsp. lime juice
- 1 tbsp. white vinegar
- 1/4 tsp. agave or honey
- Kosher salt

Directions:

1. TOSTONES
2. To peel plantains, cut 2 slits down sides of each just deep enough to go through peel, avoiding flesh; carefully peel in sections. Cut plantains crosswise 3/4 inch thick.
3. In large bowl, stir together lime juice, 2 teaspoons salt, and 4 cups water until salt dissolves. Add plantains and let soak 20 minutes.
4. Meanwhile, make dip: In blender, puree cilantro, avocado, serrano chile, garlic, scallion, lime juice, vinegar, and agave until smooth, adding 1/4 to 1/2 cup water as needed; season with salt. Press

parchment or plastic wrap directly on surface of dip and refrigerate until ready to serve.

5. Heat air fryer to 350°F. Drain plantains but do not dry (a little excess water helps soften them). In bowl, toss plantains with 1 tablespoon oil. Transfer to air fryer basket, leaving space in between, and cook 9 minutes., flipping after 5 minutes.
6. Transfer tostones to work surface lined with parchment paper. Using heavy glass or mug, firmly smash each to about 1/4 inch thick (clean bottom of glass occasionally to prevent sticking). If tostones harden, reheat briefly in air fryer for easier smashing.
7. Heat air fryer to 400°F. Using 1 tablespoon oil, brush both sides of half of tostones and sprinkle with 1/4 teaspoon salt. Transfer to air fryer basket, spacing about 1/2 inch apart, and cook until edges start to turn light golden brown, 3 to 4 minutes. Flip and cook until crisp and golden brown around edges, 4 minutes more. Transfer to plate. Repeat brushing and cooking with remaining oil and tostones and leave in air fryer.
8. When second batch is ready, top with first batch of tostones and cook until reheated and crisp, 1 to 2 minutes. Sprinkle with smoked paprika and serve immediately with dip.

Cheesy Cauliflower Arancini

Servings: 12

Cooking Time: 10 Minutes

Ingredients:

- 2 italian chicken sausage links, any casing removed
- 4 ½ cups frozen cauliflower rice
- ½ teaspoon salt
- 1 ½ cups marinara sauce
- 1 cup freshly grated mozzarella cheese
- olive oil spray for spritzing
- 2 large eggs
- ½ cup seasoned bread crumbs
- 2 tablespoons freshly grated parmesan cheese
- Equipment
- air fryer

Directions:

1. Heat a large skillet over medium high heat. Add the sausage and cook it, breaking it apart with a spoon

until it's in small crumbles. Cook for about 4 to 5 minutes.

2. Stir in the cauliflower rice, salt, and ½ cup of the marinara sauce. Cook the mixture over medium heat, stirring often, until the cauliflower is tender, about 6 to 8 minutes. Remove the skillet from the heat and let it cool for 5 minutes, then stir in the mozzarella cheese. Let the mixture cool slightly until it's easy to handle.

3. Scoop out ¼ cup of the mixture and form it into a ball with your hands. Place the ball on a baking sheet. Repeat this with the remaining cauliflower mixture.

4. Lightly beat the eggs in a small bowl. In another bowl, stir together the bread crumbs and grated parmesan. Take each ball and lightly dip it in the egg mixture, then roll it through the bread crumbs to coat it completely. Repeat with the remaining balls.

5. Once all the arncini are made, preheat the air fryer to 400 degrees. Spray the arancini with the cooking spray all over - this really helps to crisp them up! Once the air fryer is heated, add the arancini in the basket (you may need to do 2 batches) and cook for 9 to 10 minutes, gently flipping the arancini half way through.

6. Heat the remaining marinara sauce and serve the arancini with it immediately for dipping.

Ultimate 7-layer Dip

Servings: 10

Ingredients:

- 5 Roma tomatoes, small diced
- 1 red onion, small diced
- 1 cup cilantro, chopped
- 1 jalapeno, minced
- 4 limes, divided and juiced
- Kosher salt, to taste
- Ground black pepper, to taste
- 4 avocados, pits removed
- 5 flour tortillas (burrito size, 10-inch)
- Oil spray
- 8 ounces shredded cheddar cheese, plus more for garnish
- 1 can refried pinto beans (16 ounces), warmed
- 1 can refried black beans (16 ounces), warmed
- 2 cups shredded rotisserie chicken, warmed
- 2 cups salsa con queso, warmed
- 2 cups sour cream
- 1 bunch scallions, finely chopped, for garnish
- Chips, for serving
- Items Needed:
- Aluminum foil

Directions:

1. Toss the diced tomatoes, red onion, cilantro, jalapeno and juice of 2 limes together in a medium bowl to make the pico de gallo.

2. Season to taste with salt and black pepper. Reserve ¼ cup and set aside.

3. Mash the avocados in a medium bowl. Add the reserved ¼ cup of pico de gallo and the juice of the remaining 2 limes.

4. Season the guacamole to taste with salt and black pepper. Set aside.

5. Select the Preheat function on the Air Fryer and press Start/Pause.

6. Spray both sides of each tortilla with oil spray.

7. Cut a line through 4 tortillas, starting from the middle all the way to the right side.

8. Fold the cut tortillas into loosely shaped cones and place each one seam-side down into each corner of the preheated inner air fryer basket. The cones will unravel slightly, creating a bowl formation.

9. Sprinkle ¼ cup of cheddar cheese across the bottom of the tortilla bowl.
10. Place the 5th tortilla over the cheddar cheese.
11. Trim the tortillas sticking out of the corners of the air fryer basket, lining them up with the edges of the basket.
12. Lay an aluminum foil sheet down into the air fryer basket on top of the tortilla bowl, then place several balls of foil on top to help it retain its shape while cooking.
13. Place another sheet of foil on top of the foil balls and against the tortilla walls, creating a tent to prevent the air fryer balls from floating up while cooking.
14. Insert the basket into the preheated air fryer.
15. Set temperature to 400°F and time to 5 minutes, then press Start/Pause.
16. Remove the air fryer basket and place onto a heatproof surface when done cooking.
17. Detach the inner air fryer basket and carefully remove the foil tent and foil balls. Let cool completely.
18. Transfer the tortilla bowl to a serving plate.
19. Layer the refried pinto beans, refried black beans, pico de gallo, guacamole, shredded chicken, salsa con queso, and sour cream in order into the tortilla bowl.
20. Garnish with cheddar cheese and scallions.
21. Serve immediately with chips.

Air Fryer Jalapeno Poppers

Servings: 4

Cooking Time: 8 Minutes

Ingredients:
- 8 jalapeno peppers
- 6 ounces herb & garlic cream cheese or Boursin
- ¾ cup sharp cheddar cheese shredded
- 4 tablespoons bacon bits or 4 slices bacon cooked and crumbled
- ⅓ cup Panko breadcrumbs
- 1 tablespoon butter melted

Directions:
1. Preheat the air fryer to 400°F.
2. In a small bowl combine Panko, bacon and melted butter. Set aside.
3. Slice the jalapenos in half lengthwise and scrape out the seeds. Use gloves or wash your hands well afterward.
4. Combine cream cheese and shredded cheddar together in a bowl. Fill jalapenos with the cheese mixture.
5. Sprinkle each jalapeno with the Panko and bacon topping, lightly pressing to adhere.
6. Air fry for 7-9 minutes or until cheese is melted and jalapenos are tender crisp.
7. Cool at least 5 minutes before serving.

Notes

It is recommended to wear gloves while working with the jalapenos.

Air Fryer Mini Pizzas

Servings: 4

Cooking Time: 4 Minutes

Ingredients:
- 1 can Grand's biscuits
- 1 cup marinara sauce
- 10 pepperoni slices
- 8 ounces mozzarella cheese shredded
- 1/2 teaspoon olive oil

Directions:
1. Open the package of biscuits and separate each biscuit into two layers.
2. Roll each piece of biscuit out into a 4-inch circle of dough.
3. Top each piece of dough with about 1 teaspoon of marinara sauce.
4. Add pepperoni to the sauce and put freshly shredded mozzarella cheese on top of the pizzas.
5. Spray the air fryer basket with non-stick cooking spray, olive oil spray, or line with parchment paper.
6. Carefully place 2-4 of the mini pizzas into the air fryer basket, leaving an inch or more of space between each pizza.
7. Air fry the mini pizzas at 400° Fahrenheit (200 degrees Celcius) for 4 minutes, or until the pizzas have a golden brown crispy crust. Add additional cooking time if needed.
8. Carefully remove the air fried biscuit pizzas from the air fryer basket and allow them to cool slightly on a cooling rack.

9. Repeat the cooking process with the remaining pizzas.
10. Serve immediately.

Notes

This recipe was made with a 1700 watt basket style Cosori 5.8 air fryer. All air fryers cook a little differently. You may need to adjust the cooking time according to your brand of air fryer. The size and power output of your air fryer may be different, and you should check on your dish frequently the first time you make it to see if it is cooking faster or slower and if you need to add or take away cook time.

Garnish the pizzas with all of your favorite pizza toppings and serve sprinkled with fresh parmesan cheese and fresh chopped basil.

Play with additional toppings such as ground beef, mushrooms, peppers, pineapple, and more.

Ratatouille & Persian Feta Filo Parcels

Cooking Time: 1 Hour

Ingredients:
- 2 green shallots, thinly sliced
- 2 large zucchini, cut into 1cm pieces
- 1 red capsicum, deseeded, cut into 1cm pieces
- 1 large eggplant, cut into 1cm pieces
- 1 garlic clove, finely chopped
- 2 tbsp olive oil
- 2 tsp plain flour
- 1/4 cup chopped fresh continental parsley
- 2 tbsp sherry vinegar or red wine vinegar
- 12 sheets filo pastry
- 100g butter, melted, cooled
- 100g Persian feta, crumbled
- Basil pesto, to serve
- Rocket, to serve
- Select all ingredients

Directions:
1. Preheat the oven to 220C/200C fan forced. Place the shallot in a large bowl. Add zucchini, capsicum, eggplant, garlic and oil. Season and toss to combine. Transfer to a baking tray and bake for 15 minutes. Stir and bake for a further 5 minutes or until vegetables are tender and pale golden.

2. Sprinkle flour over vegetables and stir to combine. Stir in parsley and vinegar. Set aside to cool.

3. Reduce oven to 180C/160C fan forced. Line a baking tray with baking paper. Place a sheet of filo pastry on a clean work surface and brush with a little butter. Layer with another 2 filo sheets and a little more butter. Fold the stack in half widthways. Brush with a little butter. Spoon one-quarter of the ratatouille into the centre. Make a small well in the mixture. Place one-quarter of the feta in the well. Bring the sides of the pastry into the centre, scrunching gently to partially enclose filling. Repeat to make 3 more parcels.

4. Transfer parcels to prepared tray. Bake for 35-40 minutes or until golden. Cool slightly. Drizzle with pesto and serve with rocket.

Air Fryer Frozen Taquitos

Servings: 4

Cooking Time: 6 Minutes

Ingredients:
- 8 taquitos
- salsa & sour cream for serving optional

Directions:
1. Preheat air fryer to 400°F.
2. Place taquitos in a single layer in the air fryer basket.
3. Cook for 5-6 minutes or until they are heated through.

Notes
Nutrition:
- information is for taquitos only.
- Air Fryers can vary by brand, check your taquitos early to make sure they don't overcook.
- Do not overcrowd the air fryer.
- Preheat the air fryer for best results.
- Cook in batches if needed and add all taquitos to the air fryer to reheat before serving.
- You can make your own homemade taquitos by rolling your favorite fillings in small tortillas. Be sure to oil the outside well.

Sweet Potato Wedges

Servings: 6

Cooking Time: 23 Minutes

Ingredients:

- 3 medium sweet potatoes
- 2 tablespoons extra virgin olive oil
- 1 teaspoon kosher salt plus additional for serving
- 1 teaspoon garlic powder
- 1/4 teaspoon chipotle chile powder use less if sensitive to spice or omit
- ¼ teaspoon ground black pepper
- ¼ teaspoon dried rosemary

Directions:

1. Place a rack in the center of your oven and preheat the oven to 450 degrees F.
2. Scrub and dry the sweet potatoes. Peel them if you like (I leave the peels on sweet potatoes).
3. Cut each sweet potato in half lengthwise. Cut each half into 3 or 4 long spears (so you will have 6 to 8 wedges per potato). Each spear should be about ¾-inch to 1-inch wide; the most important thing is to cut them as uniform in size as you can so that they bake evenly.
4. Place the spears on a rimmed baking sheet and drizzle with the oil.
5. In a small bowl, stir together the salt, garlic powder, chipotle chile powder, black pepper, and rosemary. Sprinkle over the potatoes and toss to coat, ensuring the wedges are evenly coated with the oil and spices.
6. Arrange the sweet potato wedges into a single layer, being careful that the wedges do not touch (if your pan is crowded and they are touching, divide the wedges between two baking sheets and bake in the upper and lower thirds of the oven instead).
7. Bake the sweet potato wedges for 15 minutes, then turn over with a spatula. Return the pan to the oven and bake for another 5 to 10 minutes, until lightly browned and tender when pierced with a fork.
8. Turn the oven to broil. Broil the sweet potatoes for 3 to 5 minutes, until they are crisped at the edges to your liking (watch carefully so that they do not burn). Remove from the oven and immediately sprinkle with a pinch of additional salt. Enjoy!

Notes

TO STORE: Refrigerate sweet potato wedges in an airtight storage container for up to 4 days.

TO REHEAT: Rewarm leftovers on a baking sheet in the oven at 350 degrees F.

TO FREEZE: Freeze wedges in an airtight freezer-safe storage container for up to 3 months. Let thaw overnight in the refrigerator before reheating.

Air-fryer Sausage Pizza

Servings: 4

Ingredients:

- 1 loaf (1 pound) frozen bread dough, thawed
- 1 cup pizza sauce
- 1/2 pound bulk Italian sausage, cooked and drained
- 1-1/3 cups shredded part-skim mozzarella cheese
- 1 small green pepper, sliced into rings
- 1 teaspoon dried oregano
- Crushed red pepper flakes, optional

Directions:

1. On a lightly floured surface, roll and stretch dough into four 4-in. circles. Cover; let rest for 10 minutes.
2. Preheat air fryer to 400°. Roll and stretch each dough into a 6-in. circle. Place 1 crust on greased tray in air-fryer basket. Carefully spread with 1/4 cup pizza sauce, 1/3 cup sausage, 1/3 cup cheese, a fourth of the green pepper rings and a pinch of oregano. Cook until crust is golden brown, 6-8 minutes. If desired, sprinkle with red pepper flakes. Repeat with remaining ingredients.

Pear Wontons

Ingredients:

- 2 Bartlett pears
- 1/2 cup honey
- 1 tsp ground cinnamon
- 1 package wonton wrappers
- Water, for sealing
- 2 Tbsp unsalted butter, melted
- 1/4 cup mascarpone cheese
- 1 Tbsp honey
- 1/2 tsp ground cinnamon

Directions:

1. Core and chop the pears into small bite size pieces and add to a medium bowl.
2. Add about 1/2 cup honey and 1 tsp cinnamon to the pears and mix. Set aside.
3. Assemble the wonton by adding a teaspoon of the pears to the center.
4. Dip your fingers into some water and wet all four edges.
5. Fold into a triangle shape. Press and pinch the edges together to seal.
6. Continue this process until all the pears or wonton wrappers are gone.
7. Fill your air fryer basket, making sure not to overlap them.
8. Melt 2 Tablespoons of butter and brush on top of each wonton.
9. Air fry at 350F for minutes, or until crispy.
10. While those are cooking, make the dip. Mix the mascarpone cheese, 1 Tbsp honey and 1/2 tsp cinnamon together.
11. You can simply dip these into the mascarpone cheese mixture or you can elevate them by adding a scoop onto each wonton and top with chopped pecans!
12. ENJOY!

Air Fryer Pizza Sliders

Servings: 12

Cooking Time: 5 Minutes

Ingredients:

- 12 Slider rolls 4 English muffins can be substituted
- 1/2 cup pizza sauce
- 12 slices provolone cheese
- 1/2 cup mozzarella cheese
- 2 ounces pepperoni
- 1 teaspoon Italian seasoning

Directions:

1. Cover solid tray from toaster oven tightly with foil. Split Hawaiians nearly in half to make an open faced sandwich.
2. Spread pizza sauce on rolls. Add a layer of sliced cheese and then cover with additional shredded cheese if desired
3. Arrange pepperoni and other toppings on pizza sliders.
4. Sprinkle Italian seasong on top and bake for about 5 minutes at 350°F on the convection bake setting in an air fryer/toaster oven. Mini pizzas are ready when cheese is melted.°

Notes

Substitutions are fine - pizza sauce is about the only ingredient I haven't substituted and enjoyed the result over the years

I enjoy pizza blend cheese with is a blend of white cheeses like mozzarella and provolone, but my son loves a cheddar blend

When available adding a layer of sliced provolone cheese will really step up the flavors of this dish

Toasting the bread or crust before topping with cheese and desired Ingredients:

Mushrooms, onions and peppers taste great as optional toppings

Pepperoni can be substituted for hard salami, cooked and crumbled sausage and bacon are delicious too

Cover baking tray tightly with foil for easier cleanup

Serve open-faced or make a sandwich, whichever is easier or more fun for you to eat

SNACKS & APPETIZERS RECIPES

Air Fryer Honey Roasted Chickpeas

Ingredients:

- 8 oz canned chickpeas, drained and rinsed
- 1 ½ tsp coconut oil, melted
- 2 Tbsp honey
- ½ tsp cinnamon
- ½ tsp nutmeg
- ½ ground clove
- ½ tsp cayenne pepper
- Pinch of salt

Directions:

1. Place chickpeas in air fryer basket. Drizzle and toss with coconut oil.
2. Roast for 15 minutes at 375°F for 15 minutes. For best results, shake at least once during the cooking cycle.
3. While the chickpeas are roasting, combine remaining ingredients and mix well. Gently toss hot chickpeas in the honey mixture.
4. Return to air fryer basket and bake for an additional 3 minutes. Cool completely before serving. Enjoy!

Roasted Pumpkin Seeds

Servings: 4-6

Cooking Time: 10-30 Minutes

Ingredients:

- 1 large jack o' lantern pumpkin, or other pumpkin or squash
- 1 tbsp vegetable oil
- ½ tsp salt or 1–2 tsp of your favourite seasoning mix, such as Cajun, BBQ or fajita

Directions:

1. With a small, sharp knife, cut the top off the pumpkin and use a large spoon to scrape out the stringy pith and seeds into a bowl. Separate the seeds from the pith as best you can and put the seeds into a sieve or colander, removing as much pith as you can. Discard the pith.
2. Preheat the oven to 200C/180C Fan/Gas 6.
3. Rinse the seeds well, picking off any bits of pith and pumpkin flesh. (The pumpkin tends to stick to your hands, so a good technique for cleaning the seeds is to run your hands through the seeds and rinse them clean of pumpkin bits a couple of times.) Drain well, then spread out on a clean tea towel and pat dry.
4. Transfer the seeds to a large baking tray (or use two, so that the seeds are well spread out) and drizzle them with oil. Sprinkle with salt or seasoning mix and give them a good stir so that they are all coated.
5. Roast in the oven for 15–20 minutes, stirring them halfway through, until the seeds are toasted and golden brown. Leave to cool on the tray, then pour into a bowl to serve. They will crisp up as they cool, so don't try to eat them too soon!
6. Recipe Tips
7. You can make this at any time of year, using the seeds from any type of pumpkin or squash.
8. The roasted seeds will keep for a day or so in an airtight container, but they tend to become chewy over time.
9. To make pumpkin seeds in the air fryer, preheat the machine to 180C. Add the unoiled pumpkin seeds to the basket and cook for 1 minute to dry them. Tip them into a bowl and coat with oil, salt and spices (if using). Return them to the basket and cook for a further 3-4 minutes or until golden-brown. Tip onto a plate and allow to cool and crisp up before eating.

Blue Cheese Dressing

Servings: 1

Ingredients:

- ½ cup sour cream
- ⅓ cup mayonnaise
- 1 tablespoon fresh lemon juice
- ½ teaspoon garlic powder
- ⅓ cup blue cheese finely crumbled, divided
- 4-6 tablespoons milk or buttermilk
- salt & pepper to taste
- 1 tablespoon fresh chives optional

Directions:

1. Combine sour cream, mayonnaise, lemon juice, garlic powder, and half of the blue cheese in a blender or food processor.
2. Blend until smooth.

3. Stir in remaining blue cheese and chives if using.
4. Add milk a little at a time to reach desired consistency. Refrigerate at least 2 hours before serving.
5. Store in the refrigerator up to 1 week.

Air-fryer Nuts

Servings: 3

Cooking Time: 35 Minutes

Ingredients:
- 1 free range egg white
- 2 tsp smoked paprika
- 3/4 tsp cayenne pepper
- 2 tsp sea salt flakes
- 1 tbs caster sugar
- 500g unsalted mixed nuts

Directions:
1. Preheat a 7-litre air fryer to 150°C for 3 minutes.
2. Whisk egg white in a large bowl until frothy. Stir in paprika, cayenne pepper, salt and sugar until combined. Add nuts. Stir to coat.
3. Carefully pull out air-fryer pan and basket and place nuts in basket. Slide pan and basket back into appliance. Cook nuts for 4 minutes, stirring halfway through cooking time, or until nuts are golden and toasted. Transfer to a tray to cool.

Air Fryer Sweet Potato Fries

Servings: 4

Cooking Time: 10 Minutes

Ingredients:
- 2 medium sweet potatoes washed and sliced
- 1 tablespoon olive oil
- 1/2 teaspoon salt
- 1/2 teaspoon pepper
- 1/2 teaspoon smoked paprika

Directions:
1. Wash and peel the sweet potatoes. Pat them dry then slice them into fries.
2. In a mixing bowl, add the potatoes and toss through the oil. Add the salt, pepper, and smoked paprika, and rub over the fries.
3. Place the sweet potato fries in the air fryer basket.

4. Air fry the potatoes at 200C/400F for 10 minutes, tossing halfway through.
5. Remove the potatoes from the air fryer and serve with dipping sauce.

Notes

Serve fries with a sweet potato fry dipping sauce.

TO STORE: Leftovers can be stored in the refrigerator, covered, for up to three days.

TO FREEZE: Place the cooked and cooled fries in a ziplock bag and store them in the freezer for up to 6 months.

TO REHEAT: Either in a preheated oven or in the air fryer.

How To Make Parmesan Asparagus Fries

Servings: 4

Cooking Time: 15 Minutes

Ingredients:
- 1 pound asparagus (about 20, tough ends snapped off (look for thicker spears))
- 2/3 cup seasoned panko crumbs (or gluten-free seasoned panko)
- 2/3 cup shredded Parmesan cheese ((or dairy-free Parmesan such as Follow Your Heart))
- 2 tablespoons all-purpose flour (or gluten-free flour (such as cup4cup))
- 2 large eggs (beaten)
- olive oil spray

Directions:
1. Combine breadcrumbs and Parmesan in a large shallow bowl.
2. Place egg and flour in another shallow bowl and whisk well.
3. Dip asparagus in the egg mixture, then the panko-parmesan and spray generously with olive oil.
4. Air Fryer Directions:
5. Place in air fryer basket in an even layer and air fry 380F 6 to 7 minutes, flipping halfway until golden and tender.
6. Oven Directions:
7. To bake, preheat the oven to 425F.
8. Spray a sheet pan with oil, and place breaded asparagus on the sheet pan.

9. Spray with oil and bake 12 to 14 minutes, turning halfway, until golden and tender.

Cool Ranch Chickpeas

Servings: 6

Ingredients:

- 2 (15-oz.) cans chickpeas, drained and rinsed
- 1/2 c. extra-virgin olive oil
- 2 tbsp. ranch seasoning

Directions:

1. FOR OVEN:
2. Preheat oven to 400°F and drychickpeas very well with paper towels.Spread out chickpeas on a large bakingsheet in an even layer. Bake until goldenand crisp, 30 minutes.
3. Carefully transfer hot chickpeas toa large bowl. Using a spatula, tosschickpeas with oil and ranch seasoning.Spread out again on the baking sheetand bake for 5 minutes more.
4. Let chickpeas cool on the baking sheet.
5. FOR AIR FRYER:
6. Dry chickpeas very well with paper towels. In a large bowl, toss chickpeas with oil and seasoning.
7. Cook at 390° until golden and crisp, about 15 minutes.

Air Fryer Pasta Chips

Servings: 1

Cooking Time: 10 Minutes

Ingredients:

- 1 pound bowtie pasta
- 3 tablespoons olive oil
- 1/4 cup grated Parmesan cheese
- 1 teaspoon Italian seasoning
- 1 teaspoon garlic powder
- 1 teaspoon crushed red pepper

Directions:

1. Bring a large pot of salted water to a boil.
2. Add pasta and cook according to box directions until al dente.
3. Drain pasta and add to a large mixing bowl.
4. Add olive to pasta and toss.
5. Add in grated Parmesan cheese, Italian seasoning, garlic powder, and crushed red pepper.
6. Toss to combine.

7. Preheat air fryer to 400 degrees F.
8. Add pasta to preheated air fryer, covering the bottom of the basket and not overlapping in the basket.
9. Cook for 4 minutes on 400 degrees F.
10. Toss and cook for another 4-5 minutes at 400 degrees F. until you have reached your desired crispness.
11. Continue until all pasta chips have been made.
12. Serve with marinara sauce for dipping.

Crispy Air Fryer French Fries

Servings: 4

Cooking Time: 18 Minutes

Ingredients:

- 2 russet potatoes
- 2 tablespoons olive oil
- 1 teaspoon garlic powder or to taste
- ½ teaspoon seasoned salt or to taste

Directions:

1. Scrub potatoes and peel if desired. Cut into ¼" fries.
2. Place fries in a large bowl and fill with cold water. Soak at least 30 minutes.
3. Drain well and dab fries dry with a kitchen towel.
4. Preheat the air fryer to 390°F.
5. Toss potatoes with oil, garlic powder, and seasoned salt to taste.
6. Place the potatoes in the basket and cook for 10 minutes. Shake/flip the potatoes and cook an additional 6-8 minutes or until crisp. Add additional salt to taste.

Notes

Thicker fries may need more time, thinner fries may need a bit less time. Appliances can vary but it is easy to check on the fries a couple of minutes early and add more time if needed.

To make more fries, cook several smaller batches. Once ready to serve, add all fries to the air fryer basket and cook at 390°F for 2-3 minutes or until heated through.

Crisp up leftover air fryer French fries by placing them back into a preheated air fryer for about 3-5 minutes.

Air Fryer Green Beans

Servings: 4

Cooking Time: 6 Minutes

Ingredients:
- 1 lb green beans trimmed
- 2 tablespoons olive oil
- 1/2 teaspoon salt
- 1/2 teaspoon pepper

Directions:
1. Preheat the air fryer to 190C/375F.
2. In a mixing bowl, add the trimmed beans then toss through the olive oil, salt, and pepper.
3. Add a single layer of the beans to the air fryer basket and air fry for 8 minutes, shaking halfway through. Repeat the process until all the beans are cooked.
4. Sprinkle with parmesan cheese and add a squeeze of lemon juice.

Notes

TO STORE: Leftovers can be stored in the refrigerator, covered, for up to 5 days.

TO FREEZE: Place the cooked and cooled beans in a ziplock bag and store them in the freezer for up to 6 months.

TO REHEAT: Either microwave for a few seconds or reheat in the air fryer for 1-2 minutes.

Quick Homemade Air Fryer Crispy French Fries

Servings: 4

Cooking Time: 20 Minutes

Ingredients:
- 1 pound (454 g) fresh potatoes , cut into 1/4" french fry size
- 2 teaspoons (10 ml) olive oil
- kosher salt , to taste
- 1/4 teaspoon (1.25 ml) garlic powder , optional
- ground black pepper , to taste
- EQUIPMENT
- Air Fryer

Directions:
1. Wash and cut potatoes into french fry sizes. NOTE: Try to keep them as evenly sized as possible for even cooking.
2. Add potatoes to bowl. Drizzle olive oil evenly over the potatoes. Sprinkle salt and pepper (and/or garlic powder) evenly over potatoes.
3. Gently toss the potatoes to evenly coat with oil and seasonings. Place the potatoes in air fryer basket and spread them evenly over the basket or rack.
4. Air fry potatoes at 380°F/193°C for about 18-22 minutes. About halfway through cooking, shake the basket and gently turn the potatoes. Try not to break them. For crisper potatoes, shake them a second time and cook for an additional 2-4 minutes.
5. Serve with ketchup or your favorite dip. Enjoy!

Notes

Recipes were cooked in 3-4 qt air fryers. If using a larger air fryer, the recipe might cook quicker so adjust cooking time.

If cooking in multiple batches, the first batch will take longer to cook if Air Fryer is not already pre-heated.

Remember to set a timer to shake/flip/toss the food as directed in recipe.

Air Fryer Onion Rings

Servings: 4-6

Cooking Time: 10 Minutes

Ingredients:

- 1 large sweet (Vidalia) onion, sliced into ½-inch rings
- 2 large eggs
- ⅔ cup buttermilk
- ⅔ cup all-purpose flour
- ½ teaspoon kosher salt
- ½ teaspoon black pepper
- ½ teaspoon garlic powder
- 1 ½ cups panko bread crumbs

Directions:

1. Peel onion and cut it into ½-inch thick slices. Separate the slices and place them on a plate. Set aside.
2. In a wide, shallow bowl, lightly beat the eggs with the buttermilk until well combined. In a second bowl, combine the flour, salt, pepper, and garlic powder. Place the panko bread crumbs in a third bowl.
3. Dip each onion ring into the flour, then the buttermilk mixture, and then dredge it through the bread crumbs, pressing to adhere. Set aside on a baking sheet and repeat with remaining rings. Spray the rings with an EVO Oil sprayer.
4. Preheat the air fryer to 380 degrees F.
5. Transfer the rings into the air fryer basket in a single layer, nesting the smaller ones inside the larger ones but leaving a little space between each ring. Don't overcrowd the basket, and work in batches if necessary.
6. Air fry for 9-12 minutes, or until golden brown and crispy.
7. Sprinkle with salt if desired, and serve.

Notes

HOW TO REHEAT ONION RINGS IN THE AIR FRYER:

Preheat your air fryer to 350 degrees.

Place the leftover onion rings in the air fryer and cook for 2 to 3 minutes until warmed thoroughly and crispy.

Air Fryer Ravioli

Servings: 2

Cooking Time: 6 Minutes

Ingredients:

- 12 frozen ravioli
- 1/2 cup buttermilk*
- 1/2 cup Italian breadcrumbs
- ALSO
- Marinara sauce for dipping
- Oil for spritzing

Directions:

1. Preheat air fryer to 400 degrees.
2. Place two bowls side by side. Put the buttermilk in one and breadcrumbs in the other.
3. Dip each piece of ravioli into the buttermilk then breadcrumbs, making sure to coat it as best as possible.
4. Place each breaded ravioli into the air fryer in one single layer and cook for 6-7 minutes, spritzing the tops with oil halfway through.
5. Remove the air fryer and enjoy immediately with marinara or freeze for up to 3 months.

Notes

*substitute buttermilk by filling a large measuring cup with 2 teaspoons of vinegar and filling it up to the 1/2 cup line. Stir, then wait 5 minutes. Now you have buttermilk!

How to Cook Frozen Fried Ravioli in the Air Fryer:

Cook ravioli in a preheated air fryer at 350 degrees for 3-4 minutes, spritzing with oil before cooking.

Air Fryer Tater Tots

Servings: 4

Cooking Time: 13 Minutes

Ingredients:
- 2 cups Tater Tots

Directions:
1. Preheat the Air Fryer to 400 degrees Fahrenheit. Prepare the air fryer basket.
2. Add the Tater Tots to the air fryer basket in a single layer.
3. Cook the Tater Tots on 400 degrees Fahrenheit for 12 minutes, tossing the tots every 4 minutes. Add an additional 1-2 minutes for crispier tots.

Notes

Serve Air Fryer Tater Tots as an appetizer or side dish. Dip Tater Tots in sauces such as ketchup, mustard, BBQ sauce, cheese sauce, and more.

Air Fryer Butternut Squash Recipe

Servings: 4-6

Cooking Time: 24-32 Minutes

Ingredients:
- 2 pounds butternut squash (1 small)
- 1 1/2 tablespoons olive oil
- 1 teaspoon kosher salt
- 1/2 teaspoon garlic powder
- 1/4 teaspoon freshly ground black pepper
- SAVORY VARIATION (OPTIONAL):
- 2 teaspoons ground cumin
- 1 teaspoon paprika
- SWEET VARIATION (OPTIONAL):
- 2 tablespoons maple syrup
- 2 teaspoons ground cinnamon

Directions:
1. Heat an air fryer to 400°F. Meanwhile, if needed, peel 1 small butternut squash, halve and remove the seeds, and cut the flesh into 1/2-inch cubes (about 5 cups). Transfer the squash to a large bowl.
2. Add 1 1/2 tablespoons olive oil, 1 teaspoon kosher salt, 1/2 teaspoon garlic powder, and 1/4 teaspoon black pepper to the squash. If making the savory variation, also add 2 teaspoons ground cumin and 1 teaspoon paprika. If making the sweet variation, also add 2 tablespoons maple syrup and 2 teaspoons ground cinnamon. Toss to coat.
3. Working in batches, add the butternut squash to the air fryer basket in a single layer. Air fry until the butternut squash is tender with browned and crispy edges, shaking the basket or tossing halfway through, 12 to 16 minutes total.
4. Transfer to a bowl and loosely tent with aluminum foil to keep warm while you air fry the remaining squash.

Recipe Notes

Make ahead: The butternut squash can be cut up to 3 days in advance and refrigerated in an airtight container.

Storage: Leftovers can be refrigerated in an airtight container for up to 4 days.

Loaded Cheese Fries

Servings: 6

Cooking Time: 30 Minutes

Ingredients:
- Fries
- 32 ounces frozen french fries or 8 cups homemade french fries
- Toppings
- 1 ½ cups cheddar cheese
- 3 tablespoons bacon cooked and crumbled, or real bacon bits
- 1 cup brown gravy homemade or packet, optional
- ½ cup sour cream
- 2 green onions thinly sliced

Directions:
1. Preheat the oven to 425°F (or cook fries in the air fryer per directions in the notes).
2. Add the fries to a rimmed baking sheet and cook for 25-30 minutes or until extra crisp, stirring after 15 minutes.
3. Once the fries are crisp, remove them from the oven and turn the broiler on to 500°F.
4. Top the fries with cheddar and bacon and place back into the oven for 1-3 minutes or until the cheese is melted.
5. Top with green onions. If using, drizzle with brown gravy and top with sour cream. Serve immediately.

Notes

Thicker fries may need more time, thinner fries may need a bit less time. Appliances can vary but it is easy to check on the fries a couple of minutes early and add more time if needed.

To make frozen fries in the air fryer, cook several smaller batches. Once ready to serve, add all fries to the air fryer basket and cook at 390°F for 10-14 minutes or until crisp. Top with cheese and bacon. Cook in the air fryer for an additional 2-3 minutes.

Air Fryer Pumpkin Seeds

Servings: 4

Cooking Time: 12 Minutes

Ingredients:

- 1 cup pumpkin seeds
- 1 Tablespoon olive oil
- 1/2 teaspoon kosher salt
- 1/2 teaspoon cinnamon
- 1 Tablespoon brown sugar

Directions:

1. Carefully remove the pulp from the pumpkin and separate the pumpkin seeds from the pulp. Boil the seeds for a few moments in a pot of boiling water to help remove the pulp. You may need to run the seeds and any pulp through running water in a colander to help remove any remaining pumpkin flesh after boiling.

2. Once the seeds have been cleaned, place the clean pumpkin seeds on a paper towel and allow them to dry.

3. Preheat the Air Fryer to 370 degrees Fahrenheit. Prepare the air fryer basket with nonstick cooking spray if needed.

4. Place the fresh pumpkin seeds in a large bowl and coat with olive oil. Once the seeds have been coated in oil, add the kosher salt and brown sugar. Toss until the seeds are fully coated.

5. Place the prepared pumpkin seeds in a single layer in the prepared air fryer basket.

6. Cook on 320 degrees Fahrenheit for 10-12 minutes, tossing the seeds halfway through cook time. Add an additional minute or two for more crispy homemade pumpkin seeds.

Notes

What seasonings can I use for airfryer roasted pumpkin seeds?

You can easily change the flavors of roasted pumpkin seeds. Try seasoning the seeds with different spices such as garlic salt, garlic powder, black pepper, pumpkin pie spice, or even add a little batch of cajun creole seasoning. There are tons of options for this great snack.

How do I store roasted pumpkin seeds?

Roasted pumpkin seeds will stay fresh for a couple of days at room temperature when stored in an airtight container. Store roasted pumpkin seeds in an airtight container in the refrigerator for up to a week.

Air-fryer Chunky Chips Recipe

Servings: 4

Cooking Time: 20 Minutes

Ingredients:

- 800g Maris Piper potatoes, peeled
- 1 tbsp groundnut or vegetable oil
- pinch of flaky sea salt

Directions:

1. Slice the potatoes lengthways into 1cm thick chips and put into a bowl of cold water for 5 mins to soak.

2. Preheat the air-fryer to 200°C.

3. Drain the chips and pat dry with kitchen roll. Toss with the oil and sea salt until evenly coated. Tip into the basket, in a roughly even layer – you may need to cook them in 2 batches.

4. Cook for 20-25 mins, shaking occasionally, until well browned.

5. Tip into a bowl, sprinkle with a little more salt and let cool for 5 mins before serving.

Spicy Halloumi Fries With Chilli Butter Sweetcorn Cobettes

Servings: 4

Ingredients:
- 2 blocks of halloumi (225g each)
- 75g plain flour
- 1 tsp sumac
- 1 tsp za'atar
- 1 lemon
- 150g natural Greek yogurt
- 2 tbsp coriander, chopped
- Cooking spray or oil
- For the chilli corn butter
- 50g butter, softened
- 2 tsp tomato ketchup
- 1 tsp honey
- 1/2 tsp rose harissa
- 4 sweetcorn cobettes
- COOKING MODE
- When entering cooking mode - We will enable your screen to stay 'always on' to avoid any unnecessary interruptions whilst you cook!

Directions:
1. Drain halloumi and pat dry. Cut into thick fries.
2. In a bowl, mix the flour and sumac, za'atar. Dip halloumi into the flour to lightly coat.
3. Insert crisper plates into both drawers. Liberally spray drawer 1 with cooking spray or oil, add halloumi and spray with oil. Insert drawer into unit.
4. Make chilli butter: In a bowl, place butter, tomato ketchup, honey and harissa, beat together till smooth. Using a pastry brush, or back of a teaspoon, brush each cobettes with butter. Reserve remaining butter by placing in cling film, form into a sausage shape, wrap and chill whilst corn is cooking. Place corn onto crisper plate in zone 2 drawer. Insert drawer into unit.
5. Select zone 1, select AIR FRY, set temperature to 200°C and time for 18 minutes. Select zone 2, select ROAST, set temperature to 180°C and time to 15 minutes. Select SYNC. START/STOP to begin.
6. When zone 1 reaches 10 minutes, rearrange halloumi fries and sweetcorn. Repeat when zone 1 reaches 6 minutes

7. Cut chilli butter into 4 and place on top of corn. Serve with halloumi topped with Greek yogurt swirled with chopped coriander

Fried Zucchini Crisps With The Best Dipping Sauce

Servings: 6

Cooking Time: 15 Minutes

Ingredients:
- Fried Zucchini Ingredients:
- 1 1/2 lbs zucchini, (2 medium/large) sliced into 1/2" thick rounds
- 1/2 cup all-purpose flour for dredging, seasoned with 1 tsp salt and 1/4 tsp black pepper
- 1 tsp fine sea salt
- 1/4 tsp freshly ground black pepper
- 2 eggs, beaten, for egg wash
- 1 1/2 cups Panko bread crumbs
- extra light olive oil, Use a higher smoke point oil for frying
- For the Garlic Aioli Sauce:
- 1/3 cup mayonnaise
- 1 medium garlic clove, pressed or grated
- 1/2 Tbsp lemon juice
- 1/4 tsp fine sea salt
- 1/8 tsp freshly ground black pepper

Directions:
1. To Make Fried Zucchini Crisps:
2. Create an assembly line: In the first bowl, mix together: 1/2 cup flour with 1 tsp salt and 1/4 tsp pepper. In the second bowl, beat two eggs with a fork. In the third bowl, add 1 1/2 cups panko bread crumbs.
3. Dredge one of your zucchini slices fully in the flour mixture, tapping off the excess.
4. Next, use a fork to dip floured zucchini in the beaten egg mixture, turning to fully coat, and let the excess egg drip back into the bowl before transferring to breadcrumbs.
5. Move the zucchini to the bread crumbs bowl and coat all sides of the zucchini with crumbs. It helps to scoop the breading on top of the zucchini pieces so they are easier to flip and coat. Transfer to a platter and repeat with the remaining zucchini rounds.

6. Heat a large, non-stick, heavy-bottomed skillet over medium heat and add about 1/4" oil (enough to generously cover the bottom). Let the oil preheat to 350°F on a thermometer or when a bread crumb sizzles in the oil then add breaded zucchini chips in batches in a single layer and saute 3 minutes per side or until golden brown on each side. If browning too quickly, reduce the heat. Once zucchini is done frying, transfer them to a rack set over paper towels and repeat with remaining zucchini. Serve warm with aioli sauce.
7. To Make Garlic Aioli Dip:
8. In a small bowl, combine 1/3 cup mayo, 1 pressed garlic clove, 1/2 Tbsp lemon juice, 1/4 tsp salt and 1/8 tsp black pepper. Stir to combine and serve.

Recipe Notes

Note: Nutrition label is an estimate for pan-fried zucchini crisps. Fat content will be lower for baked or air-fried zucchini.

Air Fryer Tortilla Chips

Servings: 2

Cooking Time: 5 Minutes

Ingredients:

- 4 6-inch corn tortillas
- Avocado or olive oil spray
- ¼-½ teaspoon kosher salt

Directions:

1. Preheat the air fryer to 350 degrees F for 5 minutes.
2. Lightly spray both sides of each tortilla with oil and sprinkle with salt. Use a pizza cutter or sharp knife to cut the tortillas into triangles (you should get 6-8 chips per tortilla).
3. Place the triangles in a single layer in the air fryer basket and air fry for 3 minutes. Open the basket and flip the chips, the cook for an additional 1-2 minutes until they're crispy and golden brown.
4. Repeat with remaining tortillas until all are cooked.

Sloppy Joe Fries

Ingredients:

- 1 large onion
- Garlic
- 1 tbsp tomato puree
- 1 lb. ground beef
- 1 tbsp thyme
- 1 tbsp oregano
- 1 tsp pepper
- 1 tsp salt

Directions:

1. Toppings:
2. Chop 1 large onion
3. Using a stovetop or pressure cooker, roast garlic topped with olive oil at 350 F
4. Smash roasted garlic into paste
5. For this recipe we used one of our pressure cookers. At this step, saute onions using olive oil.
6. After the onions have cooked a little, add the mashed garlic, tomato puree, and ground beef.
7. After meat is browned, add 1 cup of canned tomatoes and spices.
8. Set aside. Time to make the fries!
9. Fries:
10. Peel 3 russet potatoes and chop into skinny wedges
11. Coat french fries with some olive oil and salt and pepper.
12. Add coated potatoes into air fryer.
13. Cook at 400 F for 8 minutes
14. After the 8 minutes take the basket out and shake fries carefully.
15. Cook for 8 minutes at 400 F
16. Place toppings on fries and cheese (optional)
17. Enjoy

Air Fryer Crinkle Cut Fries

Servings: 4

Cooking Time: 12 Minutes

Ingredients:
- 16 ounces frozen crinkle fries
- ½ teaspoon seasoned salt

Directions:
1. Preheat the air fryer to 400°F.
2. Place fries in a single layer in the air fryer basket.
3. Cook for 10-12 minutes shaking the basket halfway through cooking.
4. Toss fries with the seasoning salt and serve.

Trader Joes Frozen Handsome Cut Potato Fries In The Air Fryer

Servings: 8

Cooking Time: 17 Minutes

Ingredients:
- 24 oz. (425 g) Trader Joes Frozen Handsome Cut Potato Fries
- Kosher salt or sea salt , to taste
- ground black pepper , to taste (optional)
- EQUIPMENT
- Air Fryer

Directions:
1. Place the frozen fries in air fryer basket and spread them evenly over the basket. If you have a large air fryer, you can cook a whole bag at a time. Otherwise just cook a half a bag per batch for best results. A single layer is best and two layers deep is about the max you should do. You don't need thaw them first or to spray any extra oil.
2. Air fry the frozen fries at 400°F/205°C for about 12-17 minutes. About halfway through cooking, shake the basket and gently turn the fries. Try not to break them. For crisper, evenly cooked fries, turn them multiples times while cooking.
3. If needed, Air Fry for additional 1-3 minutes to crisp to your preferred liking. Season with salt and pepper if desired.

Notes

No Oil Necessary. Cook Fries Frozen - Do not thaw first. Shake several times for even cooking & Don't overcrowd fryer basket.

If cooking in multiple batches, the first batch will take longer to cook if Air Fryer is not already pre-heated.

Recipes were cooked in 3-4 qt air fryers. If using a larger air fryer, the recipe might cook quicker so adjust cooking time.

Remember to set a timer to shake/flip/toss the food as directed in recipe.

Air Fried Acorn Squash

Servings: 4

Cooking Time: 20 Minutes

Ingredients:
- 1 acorn squash
- 1/4 cup (45 g) butter , melted
- 1 Tablespoon (10 g) brown sugar , or more to taste
- 1/2 teaspoon (2.5 g) kosher salt , or to taste
- Black pepper , to taste
- OPTIONAL TOPPINGS:
- melted butter
- chopped roasted nuts
- pomegranate seeds
- EQUIPMENT
- Air Fryer

Directions:
1. Trim the top & bottom off the acorn squash, and then cut the squash in half from top to bottom. Scoop out the seeds using a spoon. Lay the squash cut side down on the cutting board, and cut the squash into half rings, about 1/2-inch thick.
2. In a small bowl, combine the melted butter, brown sugar, salt and pepper. Toss the acorn squash rings in the butter mixture until well coated. Place in the air fryer basket.
3. Air Fry at 375°F for about 15-20 minutes or until tender, flipping the squash after the first 10 minutes. Remember to flip so the squash cooks evenly.
4. You can make it extra delicious by drizzling the squash with extra melted butter, chopped nuts, and pomegranate seeds. Taste for seasoning and add a little more salt & pepper if desired.

BREAKFAST & BRUNCH RECIPES

Air Fryer Cheese & Ham Croissant

Ingredients:

- Croissant
- Ham
- Mayonnaise
- Cheese of choice

Directions:

1. Cut the croissant in half
2. Butter the croissant using butter or mayonnaise
3. Layer the ham, followed by cheese.
4. On top butter again with mayonnaise and sprinkle with cheese on top.
5. Air Fry for 3 minutes at 170C and cheesy cheesy, enjoy!

Gluten Free Bread Rolls

Servings: 9

Ingredients:

- 1 1/4 cup whole milk
- 36g salted butter
- 1/4 cup granulated sugar
- 10g or 1 packet of Instant yeast
- 1 egg, room temperature
- 1/4 tsp. salt
- 1 level tsp. Xanthan Gum
- 3 1/4 cup GF free flour with Xanthan Gum
- Melted butter for when they are done baking

Directions:

1. Warm the milk, butter and sugar over a slow heat. once the butter has melted and the sugar has dissolved, remove from the heat. The milk should not even simmer, so keep stirring to avoid this, once it's done, remove from the heat.
2. When you can touch the milk, with your knuckle and it doesn't burn you at all, it should be warm and not hot, add in the yeast, give it a good whisk to combine everything and set aside for 10 minutes. The yeast should foam up and look very frothy. If it does not foam up, you will have to do this again (sorry!).
3. Add the flour, salt and xanthan gum to a stand mixer (can also be done by hand) which the dough attachment, allow it to blend everything together/ or whisk the ingredients together beforehand. Then add the milk mixture and egg to the dry ingredients and mix on a medium speed.
4. Preheat the airfryer on 50 degrees C for 2 minutes, line the base of the Instant Vortex/airfryer with parchment paper and grease with olive oil or grease spray, then switch off and leave the airfryer open so it isn't too hot when you add the rolls in.
5. Once the dough is smooth and there are no lumps (mix for about 5-7 minutes while also scraping down the sides), use a measuring cup (mine is a 1/4 measuring cup) scoop out the dough, use the olive oil or water to form a ball. I also used my counter to roll it out, it helps as the dough is very sticky.
6. Place the dough balls in the airfryer (switched off) grease the tops with more olive oil, place a layer of cling wrap on top, just lightly, close the airfryer door and allow them to rise for 45 minutes.
7. Once the dough has risen, set the airfryer to 174C and bake for 10 minutes.
8. Once they are out of the oven, grease with melted butter and enjoy!

Air Fryer Hard-boiled Eggs

Servings: 1 To 6

Ingredients:

- Deselect All
- 1 to 6 large eggs

Directions:

1. Preheat a 3.5-quart air fryer to 270 degrees F. Add the eggs to the fryer basket and cook 15 minutes for hard-boiled eggs. Remove the eggs and plunge them into an ice bath. Peel when cool enough to handle.
2. For soft-boiled eggs, cook them 10 minutes. For medium-boiled eggs cook for 12 minutes.

Air Fryer Breakfast Frittata

Servings: 2

Cooking Time: 6 Minutes

Ingredients:

- 3 eggs
- 1/4 bell pepper diced
- 1/4 small onion chopped
- 2 cremini mushrooms
- salt and pepper to taste
- 2 tbspn cream or milk
- 2 tbspn shredded cheese like cheddar or any

Directions:

1. Whisk eggs with cream. Add salt and pepper. Add veggies.
2. Preheat air fryer to 400 degrees.
3. Pour the mixture to the pan and place that into the air fryer. Cook for 5 minutes.
4. Add shredded cheese and then cook for another 1 minute.
5. Carefully remove the pan from the air fryer (i used a towel) and serve with avocado, tomatoes and bread if desired. Enjoy.

Air Fryer Banana Bread

Servings: 1

Cooking Time: 30 Minutes

Ingredients:

- 2 ripe bananas, medium in size
- 120g butter, softened
- 100g caster sugar
- 200g self-raising flour
- 2 medium eggs, beaten
- 1tsp baking powder
- 1tsp ground cinnamon

Directions:

1. Mix together the butter and sugar until they are smooth. Then slowly add the beaten eggs and mix until they are combined.
2. Add the flour, baking powder and ground cinnamon, followed by the mashed bananas.
3. Stir everything together gently until combined.
4. Transfer the mixture to a greased baking tin and place it in the air fryer at 160°C. Set the timer for 30 minutes.

5. At the end of the cooking time, the banana bread should be browned on the outside and cooked all the way through. Insert a metal skewer to check it isn't wet or soggy on the inside. If it needs to be cooked for longer, check on it every 5 minutes to ensure it doesn't burn. If the outside is already browned, you might need to cover it in some foil.

Frozen Pot Pie In Air Fryer

Servings: 2

Cooking Time: 25 Minutes

Ingredients:

- 2 Frozen Pot Pies 10 ounce Chicken, Beef, or Veggie

Directions:

1. To make air fryer pot pie, begin by removing the pot pie from it's packaging and cover the pie with aluminum foil, folding the foil over the sides of pie.
2. Place the pot pie in the air fryer basket and air fry at 400 degrees F for 20-25 minutes.
3. Remove the foil, and continue to air fry for an additional 3-5 minutes, until you have golden brown crust.

Air Fryer Cinnamon Rolls

Servings: 8

Cooking Time: 8 Minutes

Ingredients:

- For the dough
- 1 3/4 cups self rising flour
- 1 cup vanilla yogurt Greek, coconut, or soy
- For the filling
- 2 tablespoons butter melted

1/4 cup brown sugar * See notes

- 2 teaspoons cinnamon
- For the frosting

2 oz cream cheese softened ** See notes

2 tablespoons butter softened ** See notes

6 tablespoons powdered sugar *** See notes

Directions:

1. In a large mixing bowl, add the flour and yogurt and mix well, until combined. If the dough is too thick, add more yogurt. If the dough is too thin, add more flour.
2. Lightly flour a kitchen surface and transfer the dough on top. Gently knead it several times, before

rolling out into a large rectangular shape, around 1/2 an inch in thickness.

3. In a small bowl, add the melted butter, brown sugar, and cinnamon. Using a spatula, spread the cinnamon mixture on top, reserving half an inch around the sides.

4. Beginning at the long end of the dough, tightly roll up the dough into a log. Use a sharp knife to slice the log into eight portions.

5. Place 3 or 4 of the cinnamon rolls into an air fryer basket lined with parchment paper. Air fry at 180C/350F for 7-8 minutes, until the edges are lightly golden brown.

6. Remove the cinnamon rolls from the air fryer basket. Add remaining cinnamon rolls and repeat the process until they are all air fried.

7. Let the cinnamon rolls cool slightly, before adding the frosting. To make the frosting, add the cream cheese and butter in a mixing bowl. Beat together until combined. Add the powdered sugar and mix until smooth.

Notes

* Coconut sugar, white sugar, or a brown sugar substitute work.

** Dairy free butter and cream cheese work.

*** Or sugar free powdered sugar.

TO STORE: Leftover air fried cinnamon rolls can be stored in the refrigerator, covered, for up to three days.

TO FREEZE: Place the rolls in an airtight container and store them in the freezer for up to two months.

TO REHEAT: Microwave the rolls for 20 seconds or reheat in the air fryer for 2-3 minutes.

Air Fryer Monkey Bread

Servings: 12

Cooking Time: 20 Minutes

Ingredients:

- 1 can biscuit dough
- 1/4 cup granulated white sugar
- 1/4 cup brown sugar
- 1 1/2 cups powdered sugar
- 5 tbsp heavy cream
- 1/2 tsp vanilla flavoring

Directions:

1. Preheat the Air Fryer to 320 degrees Fahrenheit.

2. Cut the biscuit dough into small pieces. Add the biscuit dough to a large plastic sealable bag. Add the granulated sugar and the brown to the biscuits, seal the bag closed, and then toss the bag to cover the dough in sugar.

3. Prepare a small bundt pan. Place the biscuit dough pieces into the bundt pan. Add the bundt pan to the basket of the air fryer and cook for 18-20 minutes.

4. Make the glaze while the monkey bread is baking. Add the powdered sugar, heavy cream, and vanilla flavoring to a small mixing bowl. Mix until the consistency is that of a glaze. Add more heavy cream if you would like a thinner glaze.

5. Remove the monkey bread from the air fryer once it's finished cooking. Set the bread aside and allow it to cool for 5 minutes. After 5 minutes, flip the monkey bread out of the bundt pan onto a serving plate and then top it with the homemade glaze.

6. Serve warm.

Notes

It's normal for the bottom of the monkey bread to be brown since it is exposed to the circulating air the most. Like nuts? Add ¼ cup chopped almonds or pecans to the biscuit dough mixture before baking.

Coronation Scotch Quails Eggs

Servings: 4

Ingredients:

- 12 quail eggs
- Iced water
- 300g good-quality pork sausage meat
- 2 tbsp fresh parsley, chopped
- 1 tsp Worcestershire sauce
- 1 tbsp onion chutney
- Salt and freshly ground black pepper
- 1 medium egg, beaten
- 50g plain flour
- 75g dried breadcrumbs
- COOKING MODE
- When entering cooking mode - We will enable your screen to stay 'always on' to avoid any unnecessary interruptions whilst you cook!

Directions:

1. Insert crisper plate into Zone 1 drawer. Place 12 whole eggs on top of crisper plate and insert drawer into unit. Select Zone 1, turn the dial to select AIR FRY, set temperature to 150°C, and set time to 5-6 minutes, depending how you want eggs cooked, soft or hard. Press the dial to begin cooking. When cooking is complete remove eggs with silicone tongs and plunge into iced water to stop eggs cooking further. Allow to cool, then peel shells off eggs and reserve.

2. In a large bowl, add the sausage meat, parsley, Worcestershire sauce and onion chutney together with plenty of seasoning and stir everything together until evenly mixed. Divide mixture into 4 balls and place between cling film. Squash one of the balls until it's as flat as possible in the cling film. Tip the flour onto a plate and season well. One at a time, lightly flour each cooked egg, then use the cling film to help roll the sausage meat around the egg to completely encase. Repeat with the remaining sausage balls and eggs.

3. Crack egg into a shallow bowl and beat with a fork. Add the breadcrumbs onto another plate.

4. Roll coated eggs in flour again, roll coated eggs in beaten egg and finally roll in breadcrumbs. Chill for 30 minutes.

5. Place eggs back in Zone 1 drawer. Spray eggs with oil. Turn the dial to select AIR FRY, set temperature to 180°C, and set time to 8-9 minutes. Press the dial to begin cooking.

6. Serve hot or cold.

Air Fryer Pop Tarts

Servings: 2-4

Cooking Time: 4 Minutes

Ingredients:

- 2 to 4 Pop Tarts (any flavor)

Directions:

1. Preheat your air fryer to 350 degrees.
2. Place your desired amount of pop tarts in the air fryer basket without overlapping them.
3. Cook for 3-4 minutes. Cook time may vary depending on the number of pop tarts in your basket and your air fryer design.
4. Remove carefully and enjoy.

Air Fryer Frozen Toaster Scramble

Servings: 1

Cooking Time: 8 Minutes

Ingredients:

- 1 Frozen Toaster Scramble
- EQUIPMENT
- Air Fryer

Directions:

1. Remove frozen toaster scrambles from package and take out of plastic wrap.
2. Place the frozen toaster scramble in the air fryer basket. If cooking multiple toaster scrambles, spread out into a single even layer. Don't overlay or else the won't cook evenly. No oil spray is needed.
3. Air Fry at 340°F/171°C for 6 minutes. Flip the toaster scramble over.
4. Continue to Air Fry at 340°F/171°C for another 1-2 minutes, or until golden and filling is heated through.

Notes

Air Frying Tips and Notes:

No Oil Necessary. Cook Frozen - Do not thaw first.

Remember to turn/flip after the first 6 minutes. Don't overcrowd the air fryer basket.

Recipe timing is based on a non-preheated air fryer. If cooking in multiple batches of hot pockets back to back, the following batches may cook a little quicker.

Recipes were tested in 3.7 to 6 qt. air fryers. If using a larger air fryer, the toaster scrambles might cook quicker so adjust cooking time.

Breakfast Bombs

Servings: 4-6

Ingredients:

- 1 tube refrigerated biscuit dough
- 1 tbsp. butter
- 4 eggs
- 2 tbsp. whole milk
- 1 tbsp. finely chopped chives
- 4 slices bacon, cooked and crumbled
- 3/4 c. shredded cheddar
- 2 tbsp. melted butter
- 1 tbsp. coarse salt
- 1 tbsp. poppy seeds (or everything seasoning)

Directions:

1. FOR OVEN
2. Preheat oven to 375°. Spray an 8" round baking pan or pie dish with cooking spray.
3. In a large nonstick skillet, melt butter over medium heat. In a large bowl, whisk together eggs and milk. Pour egg mixture in pan and let set slightly. Reduce heat to medium low, and stir occasionally until scrambled eggs reach desired consistency. Season with salt and pepper. Remove from heat and fold in chives.
4. Flatten each biscuit round to about ¼" thickness. Top each round of dough with scrambled eggs, bacon and cheese. Bring the edges of the dough together and pinch to seal. Place in pan seam side-down.
5. Brush with tops with melted butter then sprinkle with coarse salt and poppy seeds. Bake until the biscuits are golden and cooked through, about 20 to 25 minutes. Serve warm.
6. FOR AIR FRYER
7. In a large skillet over medium heat, melt butter. In a large bowl, whisk together eggs and milk. Pour egg mixture in pan and let set slightly. Reduce heat to medium-low, and stir occasionally until soft

curds form. Season with salt and pepper. Remove from heat and fold in chives.

8. Flatten each biscuit into a ¼" thick round. Top each round of dough with scrambled eggs, bacon and cheese. Bring the edges of the dough together and pinch to seal.
9. Brush with tops with melted butter then sprinkle with salt and everything seasoning.
10. Line basket of air fryer with a piece of parchment paper greased with cooking spray and, working in batches, add biscuit bombs, making sure they don't touch. Bake at 375° until biscuits are golden and cooked through, about 10 minutes.

Air Fryer Chinese Egg Rolls

Cooking Time: 20 Minutes

Ingredients:

- Filling
- 2 tablespoons peanut oil (or vegetable oil)
- 1 cup carrots , shredded
- 2 cups napa cabbage , thinly shredded
- 1 cup bean sprouts
- 3 tablespoons soy sauce
- 1 teaspoon honey
- 4 cloves garlic , minced
- 1 tablespoon ginger , minced
- 1 pound (450 grams) ground turkey (or chicken)
- 1 tablespoon hoisin sauce
- 1/4 teaspoon black pepper
- 1/3 cup green onions , thinly sliced
- Egg rolls
- 25 egg roll wrappers 6 1/2 x 6 1/2 inches or 17 x 17 cm, thawed (Footnote 1)
- Vegetable oil for deep frying
- Dipping sauce (optional)
- Homemade sweet chili sauce (or store bought)
- Chinese dumpling sauce
- Homemade hoisin sauce (or store bought)

Directions:

1. Egg roll filling
2. Heat 1 tablespoon oil in a large nonstick skillet (or cast iron skillet) over medium-high heat until hot. Add the carrot and napa cabbage. Cook and stir for 2 minutes.
3. Add the bean sprouts and stir for 1 minute.

4. Add 1 tablespoon soy sauce and the honey. Cook and stir for another minute until the liquid has evaporated. Transfer everything to a plate to cool.

5. Add the remaining 1 tablespoon of oil and the garlic and ginger into the same skillet. Stir for 20 to 30 seconds, to release the fragrance.

6. Add the ground turkey (or chicken). Cook while chopping the ground meat into small bits with a spatula, until lightly browned.

7. Add the remaining 2 tablespoons of soy sauce and the hoisin sauce and black pepper. Stir and cook until the liquid is absorbed, 2 to 3 minutes. Transfer everything to a medium-sized bowl to cool.

8. Add the cooked vegetables and green onions to the bowl of ground turkey. Stir to mix well.

9. Wrap the egg rolls

10. To prepare the wrapping station: Add some water to a small bowl. Place the egg roll wrappers on a plate along with a spoon and the filling. Prepare a large plate or oven tray to hold the wrapped egg rolls and a cutting board for wrapping the egg rolls.

11. To wrap an egg roll, gently remove one egg roll sheet from the stack using both of your hands and place it on the cutting board, with a corner pointed toward you. Add 2 to 3 tablespoons of filling onto the lower end of the wrapper, making a 4-inch (10 cm) wide, tight and even mound. Tightly roll from the bottom corner toward the top, until about halfway up. Tightly fold the left and right corners of the wrapper towards the center, so it looks like an opened envelope. Dip your finger into the water and brush the top corner of the wrapper. Tightly roll the egg rolls upward until it's completely sealed. Repeat the process, until you've used all the filling.

12. Although you can freeze the egg rolls at this stage, I personally prefer to cook them all and store the cooked ones so I only need to set up the deep frying equipment once. On the other hand, if you want to make the egg rolls in advance and serve them fresh at your party, you can freeze the egg rolls without cooking them. To do so, place the egg rolls on a baking sheet with gaps in between. Wrap them tightly with plastic wrap and store in the freezer until ready to cook. You can fry them directly from the freezer, with an additional 1 minute of fry time.

13. Cook the egg rolls

14. Prepare a baking sheet with a rack on top, for cooling the egg rolls.

15. Option 1 - To deep fry the egg rolls, heat 1-inch (2.5 cm) of oil in a deep medium pot or a dutch oven over medium heat to 350 F (177 C). If you do not have a thermometer, insert a wooden chopstick into the heated oil. You should see continuous tiny bubbles coming up around the chopstick. If the bubbles only come up here and there, the oil is not hot enough. If the bubbles are large and bursting to the surface, the oil is too hot.

16. Fry the egg rolls in batches of 5 to 6. Flip and move them occasionally for even browning. Fry until the egg rolls are golden, 5 to 6 minutes. Drain and transfer the egg rolls with a slotted spoon or wire spider onto the rack to let them cool. Repeat until you have cooked all the egg rolls.

17. Option 2 - To bake the egg rolls in the oven, preheat the oven to 400 degrees F (200 C). Place the egg rolls onto a lined baking sheet, seam-side-down, with about 2 fingers' width gap between. Generously spray oil on top. Bake for 9 minutes, or until the bottom turns a golden color. Flip the spring rolls and spray oil onto them again. Return the tray to the oven. Bake for another 6 to 8 minutes, until the other side is golden as well. Once done, let the egg rolls cool on a wire rack for 10 minutes before serving to maximize crispiness.

18. Option 3 - To fry the egg rolls in an air-fryer, preheat the air-fryer to 390 F (10 mins or so). Cook them in batches. Spread a few spring rolls in the basket without overlapping them. Spray with a thin layer of oil, or you can bake them without using any oil. Bake for 6 minutes, flip, and bake for another 5 minutes. Once done, let the egg rolls cool on a wire rack for 10 minutes before serving to maximize crispiness.

19. Serve the egg rolls hot with whichever dipping sauce(s) you prefer.

20. Store and reheat

21. You can store the cooked egg rolls and reheat them later. If stored and reheated properly, the egg rolls will be just as crispy as freshly fried.

22. To store the egg rolls, spread them on a wire rack and let them cool completely. The egg rolls will be very hot inside once cooked, so it might take 1 to 2

hours for them to cool completely. Once cooled, you can store them in an airtight container or in a large ziplock bag. To get the best result, I prefer to spread the egg rolls in a single layer in a gallon ziplock bag and lay them flat in the fridge (or freezer). This way, the egg rolls won't overlap and get soggy.

23. You can reheat the egg rolls in the oven or in an air fryer. Bake them at 350 F (180 C) until hot, or for about 10 minutes or so. The rolls will remain crispy.

Notes

The recipe was adapted from the one in Jessica Gavin's cookbook Easy Culinary Science for Better Cooking.

The nutrition facts are calculated based on 1 of the 20 egg rolls generated by this recipe, without any dipping sauce.

The best way to thaw the egg roll wrappers is to transfer the package from the freezer to the fridge and let them thaw slowly over a couple hours. If you're in a hurry, you can also place the package of egg roll wrappers on your kitchen counter for 20 to 30 minutes.

Tortilla Chips In Your Air Fryer!

Ingredients:

- corn tortillas
- olive oil
- salt, to taste

Directions:

1. Cut each tortilla into 8 triangles and lay on a flat surface. Brush the triangles lightly with olive oil and sprinkle with salt, to taste. Line your air fryer basket with perforated parchment paper (optional) and place in a single layer. Air fry at 350°F for 4 minutes.

Air Fryer Hard Boiled Eggs

Servings: 4-6

Ingredients:

- 4 large eggs
- Water and ice, for ice bath

Directions:

1. Preheat air fryer to 270°. Add eggs and cook for 15 minutes for hard boiled eggs. For eggs with jammier yolks, cook for 12 to 13 minutes; for soft boiled eggs, 9 to 10 minutes.

2. While the eggs cook, prepare an ice bath. As soon as the eggs are done, transfer them to the ice bath to halt the cooking. Once cooled, peel the eggs and serve.

Air-fryer Quesadillas

Servings: 6

Ingredients:

- 1-1/2 cups shredded Mexican cheese blend
- 1/2 cup salsa
- 4 flour tortillas (8 inches), warmed
- Cooking spray

Directions:

1. Preheat air fryer to 375°. Combine cheese and salsa; spread over half of each tortilla. Fold tortilla over. In batches, place tortillas in a single layer on a greased tray in air-fryer basket; spritz with cooking spray. Cook until golden brown and cheese has melted, 5-7 minutes. Cut into wedges.

Hot Cross Buns

Servings: 4

Cooking Time: 25 Minutes

Ingredients:

- 1 cup unbleached all purpose flour, whole wheat or gluten-free mix* ((5 oz))
- 2 teaspoons baking powder (make sure it's not expired or it won't rise)
- 2 tablespoons raw sugar
- 3/4 teaspoon cinnamon
- 1/2 teaspoon kosher salt (use less if using table salt)
- 1 cup 0% Greek yogurt (not regular yogurt, it will be too sticky)
- 3 tablespoon raisins
- 1 egg white (beaten (whole egg works fine too))
- Icing (only half will get used)*:
- 1/4 cup powdered sugar
- 1 teaspoon milk or water

Directions:

1. Oven Directions:
2. Preheat oven to 375F.
3. Place parchment paper or a silpat on a baking sheet. If using parchment paper, spray with oil to avoid sticking.
4. In a medium bowl combine the flour, baking powder, sugar, cinnamon and salt and whisk well.
5. Add the yogurt and raisins, mix with a fork or spatula until well combined, it will look like small crumbles.
6. Lightly dust flour on a work surface and remove dough from the bowl, knead the dough a few times until dough is tacky, but not sticky, about 10 to 15 turns (it should not leave dough on your hand when you pull away).
7. Divide into 8 equal balls. Place on the prepared baking sheet.
8. Top with egg wash. Bake on the top rack of the oven for 25 minutes. Let cool at least 30 minutes before icing.
9. For the icing:
10. In a small bowl, whisk the powdered sugar with milk until smooth. Transfer to a small ziplock bag and cut the tip. Ice the tops of the rolls in a cross pattern.
11. Air Fryer Directions:
12. Preheat the air fryer 325F degrees and set for 11 to 12 minutes.
13. Transfer in batches without overcrowding and bake 11 to 12 minutes, or until golden. No need to turn.
14. Let cool at least 30 minutes before icing.

Notes

*Since only half gets used on top, I deducted half of the sugar from the analysis.

Air Fryer Breakfast Bombs

Servings: 4

Ingredients:

- Olive oil cooking spray
- 3 large eggs
- 2 tsp. whole milk
- 1/4 tsp. kosher salt
- 1/4 c. cooked black beans
- 1/4 c. pico de gallo
- 1/2 c. shredded pepper Jack cheese
- All-purpose flour, for surface
- 8 oz. whole grain or whole wheat pizza dough
- Hot sauce, for serving

Directions:

1. Grease a 6" nonstick round cake pan with cooking spray. In a medium bowl, whisk eggs, milk, and salt to combine. Stir in beans and pico de gallo.
2. Pour egg mixture into prepared pan; place pan in an air-fryer basket. Cook at 300°, stirring and scraping bottom and sides every 2 minutes, until scrambled and just cooked through, 8 to 10 minutes. Remove from air fryer and stir in cheese.
3. On a lightly floured surface, divide dough into 4 pieces. Roll each piece into a thin 5" circle. Divide egg mixture among rounds (about a heaping 1/4 c. each). Bring edges of dough together; pinch to seal. Spray with cooking spray.
4. Spray air-fryer basket with cooking spray. Arrange filled dough in a single layer in basket, spacing about 1/2" apart. Cook at 350° until golden and crispy, about 10 minutes. Serve warm with hot sauce alongside.

Taco Fried Egg Rolls

Ingredients:

- 1 lb. ground beef
- 16 egg roll wrappers
- ½ onion, chopped
- 1 can Cilantro Lime Rotel
- ½ can refried black beans
- ½ packet of Taco Seasoning
- 1 cup shredded Mexican cheese
- ½ cup whole kernel corn
- 1 tbsp olive oil
- 2 garlic cloves, chopped
- Salt and pepper to taste
- 1 tsp chopped cilantro, optional

Directions:

1. In your Pressure Cooker, spray the inner pot with olive oil cooking spray. Set it on medium-high. Add in the garlic and onions, cooking until fragrant.
2. Then, add in the ground beef, salt, pepper, and taco seasoning. Cook until the meat is browned and in small chunks. Add the Rotel, beans and corn, stirring consistently.
3. Lay the egg roll wrappers on a flat surface. Dip a cooking brush in water and glaze each of the egg roll wrappers along the edges. This will soften the crust and make it easier to roll.
4. Load the mixture into each of the wrappers and fold the wrappers diagonally to close. Then, press firmly on the area with the filling and cup it to secure it in place. Fold in the left and right sides as triangles and fold the final layer over the top to close.
5. Place in the air fryer basket with perforated parchment paper (optional) and spray each egg roll with olive oil cooking spray.
6. Air fry at 400°F for 8 minutes. Flip the egg rolls after 8 minutes and cook for an additional 4 minutes. Sprinkle with cilantro and serve with the dipping sauces of your choice!

Air-fryer Crispy Sriracha Spring Rolls

Servings: 2

Cooking Time: 10 Minutes

Ingredients:

- 3 cups coleslaw mix (about 7 ounces)
- 3 green onions, chopped
- 1 tablespoon soy sauce
- 1 teaspoon sesame oil
- 1 pound boneless skinless chicken breasts
- 1 teaspoon seasoned salt
- 2 packages (8 ounces each) cream cheese, softened
- 2 tablespoons Sriracha chili sauce
- 24 spring roll wrappers
- Cooking spray
- Optional: Sweet chili sauce and additional green onions

Directions:

1. Preheat air fryer to 360°. Toss coleslaw mix, green onions, soy sauce and sesame oil; let stand while cooking chicken. Place chicken in a single layer on greased tray in air-fryer basket. Cook until a thermometer inserted in chicken reads 165°, 18-20 minutes. Remove chicken; cool slightly. Finely chop chicken; toss with seasoned salt.
2. Increase air-fryer temperature to 400°. In a large bowl, mix cream cheese and Sriracha chili sauce; stir in chicken and coleslaw mixture. With 1 corner of a spring roll wrapper facing you, place about 2 tablespoons filling just below center of wrapper. (Cover remaining wrappers with a damp paper towel until ready to use.) Fold bottom corner over filling; moisten remaining edges with water. Fold side corners toward center over filling; roll up tightly, pressing tip to seal. Repeat.
3. In batches, arrange spring rolls in a single layer on greased tray in air-fryer basket; spritz with cooking spray. Cook until lightly browned, 5-6 minutes. Turn; spritz with cooking spray. Cook until golden brown and crisp, 5-6 minutes longer. If desired, serve with sweet chili sauce and sprinkle with green onions.

Sausage Roll Wreath

Ingredients:

- 1 lb. ground sausage
- 2 Tbsp. finely chopped sage
- ¼ tsp ground cloves
- 1 tsp salt
- 1 tsp pepper
- 1 sheet puff pastry
- 1 large egg, beaten
- For the relish
- 14 oz. cranberry sauce
- Zest of 1 orange
- 1 cinnamon stick
- 1 star anise

Directions:

1. Preheat the Air Fryer Oven to 400°F.
2. In a bowl, mix the sausage, sage, ground cloves, and some salt and pepper.
3. For the relish, mix together the cranberry sauce, orange zest, star anise, cinnamon stick. Reserve 4 Tablespoons of cranberry sauce for later and warm the rest of the relish up either by microwaving or by putting it in a small saucepan.
4. Thaw the puff pastry for about 10 minutes before you need to roll it out. Roll the pastry to a long rectangle. Spread the reserved 4 tablespoons of cranberry sauce lengthways down the middle of the pastry, in a line. Mold the sausage meat mixture into a log shape and lay it on top of the cranberry sauce.
5. Use the beaten egg to brush down one side of the pastry. Fold the other side over the meat, then roll onto the egg-washed side to seal.
6. Make about 10-12 even cuts about two thirds of the way through the sausage roll, making sure not to cut all the way through.
7. Place on the Air Fryer Oven baking pan and join the two ends together to form a wreath shape. Use a little more egg wash to join the 2 ends.
8. Gently twist each piece of sausage roll over, without tearing it from the main body, so it is filling-side up. Brush any exposed pastry with the remaining egg wash.
9. Bake for about 35 minutes until the pastry is golden and puffed, and the sausage meat is cooked through.
10. Serve with the relish in a small bowl in the center for dipping and enjoy!

Easy Air Fryer Omelette

Ingredients:

- 2 eggs
- 1/4 cup milk
- Pinch of salt
- Fresh meat and veggies, diced (I used red bell pepper, green onions, ham and mushrooms)
- 1 teaspoon McCormick Good Morning Breakfast Seasoning – Garden Herb
- 1/4 cup shredded cheese (I used cheddar and mozzarella)
- Cook Mode Prevent your screen from going dark

Directions:

1. In a small bowl, mix the eggs and milk until well combined.
2. Add a pinch of salt to the egg mixture.
3. Add your veggies to the egg mixture.
4. Pour the egg mixture into a well-greased 6″x3″ pan.
5. Place the pan into the basket of the air fryer.
6. Cook at 350° Fahrenheit for 8-10 minutes.
7. Halfway through cooking sprinkle the breakfast seasoning onto the eggs and sprinkle the cheese over the top.
8. Use a thin spatula to loosen the omelette from the sides of the pan and transfer to a plate.
9. Garnish with extra green onions, optional

Air Fryer Toast

Ingredients:

- Bread
- Butter (optional)

Directions:

1. Place bread in the air fryer
2. Toast at 400 for 3 minutes. Flip and toast for an additional 2 minutes.
3. Remove from the air fryer basket, cut in half, spread some butter on it, Enjoy

Air Fryer Eggplant Recipe

Servings: 4

Cooking Time: 10 Minutes

Ingredients:

- 1 medium Eggplant (sliced)
- 2 tbsp Olive oil
- 1 tsp Sea salt
- 1/2 tsp Black pepper
- 1 cup Grated parmesan cheese
- 2 tsp Italian seasoning

Directions:

1. Preheat the air fryer to 375 degrees F (190 degrees C).
2. Slice the eggplant crosswise to make circles, about 1/2 inch (1.25 cm) thick. Cut off the leafy end only after you are done slicing, so that you'll have more to grab onto as you slice.
3. Drizzle or brush the eggplant slices with olive oil. Sprinkle with sea salt, black pepper, Parmesan cheese, and Italian seasoning.
4. Arrange eggplant slices in a single layer in the air fryer basket. Cook for 10-12 minutes, until the eggplant is soft and the cheese is golden brown. Repeat in batches with remaining eggplant slices.

Air Fried Cadbury Eggs

Servings: 4

Cooking Time: 6 Minutes

Ingredients:

- 1 can Pillsbury Crescents 8 ounces
- 4 Cadbury Crème Eggs

Directions:

1. To make these fried Cadbury eggs, begin by unwrapping each egg from their foil wrapper.
2. Open the crescent rolls and separate dough into the pre-cut triangles. Wrap one egg in each piece of pastry, making sure to completely cover the egg. Pinch the dough to cover any exposed chocolate.
3. To prepare the air fryer basket, lightly spray or line with parchment paper, to prevent sticking. Place each wrapped egg in the air fryer basket. If making multiple eggs, keep them in a single layer.
4. Air Fry at 350° Fahrenheit for 6 minutes, until they are golden brown.
5. Serve warm, or you can allow the eggs to cool so the liquid crème filling can become less gooey.

Notes

I use the Cosori 5.8 basket air fryer and 6 minutes was perfect. I did not preheat air fryer. Because all air fryers are not the same, you may need to add another minute cook time.

DESSERTS RECIPES

Halloween Candy Cookie Bars

Ingredients:

- 1 cup brown sugar
- 1 cup white sugar
- 1 cup butter, melted
- 2 eggs
- 1 tablespoon vanilla
- ½ teaspoon salt
- 2 cups flour
- 2 cups assorted candy, chopped

Directions:

1. Preheat air fryer oven to 350°F.
2. Chop your Halloween candy into bite-size pieces.
3. In a large bowl, mix sugars and melted butter and whisk.
4. Mix in eggs, vanilla, salt and flour and mix to a smooth consistency.
5. Fold in the candy pieces.
6. Grease your 8" x 8" baking dish. Pour in the mixture and smooth the top and place any remaining candy pieces on the top.
7. Bake at 350°F for 45-50 minutes.
8. Allow to cool before cutting into squares. Enjoy!

Air Fryer Oatmeal Raisin Cookies

Servings: 8

Cooking Time: 6 Minutes

Ingredients:

- 1 cup granulated sugar
- 1/2 cup unsalted butter softened
- 1 teaspoon vanilla extract
- 2 large eggs
- 1 cup all purpose flour
- 1/2 teaspoon salt
- 1/2 teaspoon baking powder
- 1/2 teaspoon cinnamon
- 1/4 teaspoon baking soda
- 1 1/2 cups oats
- 1 cup raisins

Directions:

1. In a large bowl, combine the butter and sugar. Beat together and then add eggs and vanilla. Continue mixing together until light and fluffy.
2. Add in the flour, salt, baking powder, cinnamon and baking soda. Mix until well combined.
3. Add the oats and raisins, stirring to mix thoroughly into the dough.
4. Use a scoop or large spoon to scoop a ball of dough and place into the air fryer basket, lined with air fryer parchment paper. Leave about 1 inch in between cookies for room to spread.
5. Air Fry at 300 degrees Fahrenheit for 5-6 minutes, until cookies are golden brown. Let cookies rest for 1-2 minutes before removing from air fryer basket.

Notes

When making these cookies, if you don't have room for spread, you can chill the dough for about 30 minutes before cooking.

When removing the cookies, they can be soft when warm, so letting them sit for a few minutes, helps them to slightly firm. You can lift the piece of parchment paper liner with the cookies for easier removal and then transfer them to a wire rack to continue cooling.

For a chewier cookie, substitute half brown sugar for granulated sugar.

Bloody Witch Finger Cookies

Servings: 30

Ingredients:

- 16 ounce package pre-made sugar cookie dough
- 1 cup all-purpose flour
- 3 teaspoons water
- 5 Oreo cookies, ground up into crumbs in a food processor
- ½ cup raspberry jam
- ½ cup sliced almonds

Directions:

1. Place sugar cookie dough, flour, water, and ¼ cup of the Oreo cookie crumbs in a large bowl. Knead with your hands or in a stand mixer until all the ingredients are incorporated into the dough.

2. Take 1 ½ tablespoons of dough at a time and roll the dough between your palms into a 5-inch longer finger about ¼-inch thick. Firmly press a sliced almond into the end of each finger to make fingernails. Make several horizontal cuts in the center of each finger to make knuckles. Place fingers on a wax paper lined baking sheet.

3. Select the Preheat function on the Air Fryer, adjust temperature to 320°F, and press Start/Pause.

4. Place fingers into the preheated air fryer basket. You will need to work in batches.

5. Set the temperature to 320°F, time to 7 minutes, and press Start/Pause.

6. Remove fingers when lightly golden and place on a wire rack to cool completely.

7. Heat the raspberry jam in a saucepan or microwave until gently warmed through.

8. Dip the end of each finger into the raspberry jam and place onto a serving platter.

Sweet Potato Casserole With Pecans

Servings: 8-10

Cooking Time: 50 Minutes

Ingredients:
- For the filling
- 2 1/2 pounds sweet potatoes
- 1/2 cup milk
- 1/3 cup maple syrup
- 1 large egg
- 1/2 teaspoon ground cinnamon
- 1/4 teaspoon ground ginger
- 1/4 teaspoon nutmeg
- 1/4 teaspoon kosher salt
- Zest from 1 medium orange
- For the crumble topping
- 3/4 cup chopped pecans
- 1/2 cup all-purpose flour
- 1/2 cup dark brown sugar
- 4 tablespoons unsalted butter
- 1/2 teaspoon ground cinnamon
- Special Equipment
- Food processor

Directions:
1. Preheat oven:
2. Preheat the oven to 350°F.
3. Butter a 2-quart baking dish and set aside.
4. Cook the sweet potatoes:
5. Peel the sweet potatoes and cut them into 2-inch chunks. Place the chunks in a large pot and fill it with enough water to cover the potatoes.
6. Bring everything to boil, then reduce to a simmer and cook for 15 minutes, or until the sweet potato chunks can be easily pierced with a fork. Drain the sweet potatoes and let them cool for 5 minutes.
7. Blend the sweet potatoes:
8. Working in batches, transfer sweet potatoes to a food processor and blend to make a smooth puree.
9. Makes about 4 cups of puree. (At this point, the puree can be refrigerated for several days until you're ready to make the casserole.)
10. Make the sweet potato filling:
11. Add the sweet potato puree into a large bowl. Mix in the milk, maple syrup, egg, cinnamon, ginger, nutmeg, salt, and orange zest.
12. Pour the sweet potato puree into the prepared baking dish and spread to an even layer.
13. Make the topping:
14. In a separate bowl, mix the pecans, flour, brown sugar, butter, and cinnamon together for the crumble topping. It should form large floury clumps. Sprinkle crumble over the sweet potatoes.
15. Bake:
16. Bake for 30 to 35 minutes, until the topping is a nice golden brown.
17. Let the casserole cool for 10 minutes before serving.

Bagel Bites In The Air Fryer

Servings: 4-5

Cooking Time: 10 Minutes

Ingredients:
- 12 to 15 Frozen Bagel Bites

Directions:
1. Preheat air fryer to 350 degrees F.
2. Place frozen bagel bites in your air fryer, leaving a little space around each of them.
3. Cook for 7 to 9 minutes. Every air fryer is a little different so check for doneness at 7 minutes and then continue cooking till they are golden brown.

Pistachio Cookies

Ingredients:

- 1 stick salted butter, softened
- 1/4 cup powdered (confectioners) sugar + more for coating & sprinkling
- 1 tsp vanilla
- 3/4 cups all purpose flour
- 1/2 package pistachio instant pudding mix

Directions:

1. In a large bowl, with a stand or hand mixer cream butter until smooth. Add in 1/4 cup powdered sugar and beat until fluffy. Add in vanilla and mix until combined.
2. In another bowl combine flour and dry pudding mix until combined. Gradually add flour mixture into butter mixture until it forms a dough.
3. Wrap and refrigerate for 1 hour.
4. Remove from refrigerator and use tablespoon measuring spoon to make a cookie ball. Lightly roll in powdered sugar. Take back of measuring spoon to slightly press ball.
5. Place on a baking pan and bake at 350*F for 6 minutes. Remove and let cool 3 to 5 minutes in baking pan.
6. Sprinkle more powdered sugar over the top, if desired.

Air Fryer Apple Hand Pies

Servings: 4

Cooking Time: 6 Minutes

Ingredients:

- 1 pie crust refrigerated or homemade
- 1 1/2 cups apple pie filling
- Egg Wash Mixture
- 1 large egg
- 1 tablespoon sweetened condensed milk
- Topping
- 1 tablespoon granulated sugar
- 1 teaspoon ground cinnamon

Directions:

1. Remove pie crust from the package. Unroll it onto a flat surface, such as a larger cutting board or clean kitchen counter.
2. Using a pastry cutter or sharp paring knife, cut the crust into small circles, about 6 inches in size. Then reroll the scraps of pie crust into a flat layer using a rolling pin and cut additional circles until all of the crust is used.
3. Place each 6-inch circle on a baking sheet. Spoon apple pie filling onto the center of one side of each crust circle (leaving space for edges). Once they are all filled, fold the crust over and pinch or use a fork to seal edges.
4. In a small bowl, whisk the egg and milk to make the egg wash. Then in another small dish, combine the sugar and ground cinnamon together. Brush pies with egg wash mixture onto the top of each pie and then sprinkle with sugar and cinnamon, or just coarse sugar.
5. Spray the air fryer basket with nonstick spray or line with air fryer parchment paper liners. Air fry at 380 degrees F for 6 minutes, turning pies halfway through cooking process.
6. Let them rest for a few minutes on a baking rack and then serve hot, warm or room temperature.

Notes

Optional Fillings: Some favorite fillings are blueberry, cherry, peach, strawberry or blackberry (adding a small squeeze of lemon juice will enhance the fruit flavor).

Optional Toppings: A touch of powdered sugar, caramel sauce, glaze of confectioners sugar, brown sugar or granulated sugar with fall spices. For an extra depth of flavor sprinkle flaky sea salt or homemade nutmeg salt on top of pies when hot.

Substitutions for crust: Homemade pie crusts are always great. Store bought puff pastry, pie dough circles, pizza dough or pastry rounds will also make good crusts for this dish. Any crusts from packaging will vary in cooking times.

Tips: Do not overfill pies with apple mixture or the filling will leak out into the basket. Cutting vents in top of pies will help the steam escape and create the perfect hand pie. To create an extra seal when closing the pastry, brush the edges with water.

Rooibos Cheesecake With Caramel Sauce, Salted Caramel Brittle And Apple Chips

Servings: 6-8

Ingredients:

- Cheesecake batter:
- 500g plain cream cheese
- 1/2cup sugar
- 8-10 rooibos teabags, soaked in 3-4 Tbsp of water
- 2 eggs , 1 yolk
- 1 Tbsp Vanilla extract
- Biscuit base:
- 8 ginger biscuits, crumbs
- 60g butter, melted
- Caramel brittle:
- 150g white sugar
- 4 Tbsp water
- Caramel sauce:
- 100g brown sugar
- 100g butter
- 150ml fresh cream
- Apple chips:
- 1 apple, sliced
- 1/4 tsp cinnamon

Directions:

1. Make sure all the cheesecake ingredients are at room temperature*
2. For the biscuit base:
3. Crush ginger biscuits in a food processor or in a freezer bag with a rolling pin until fine crumbs form. Place crumbs into mixing bowl and add melted butter, mix with fork until mixture sticks together.
4. Spray springform pan with baking spray, pour in the biscuit base mixture then gently press down on the base and sides, as evenly as possible. Place in the fridge to set while you make cheesecake batter.
5. For Batter
6. In a large mixing bowl, mix sugar and cream cheese until smooth. Stir in vanilla and squeeze soaked Rooibos tea bags into the mixture, mix well together then add eggs, one at a time, mixing after each addition. Pour batter into cold prepared biscuit base.
7. Place trivet rack into the bottom of the inner pot, then add 1 cup of water. Lower the cheesecake onto the rack and set to pressure cook mode on high heat for 30 mins + 10 min natural release. Once cycle is complete and pin drops, carefully open the lid and lift the cheesecake out. Allow to cool for an hour at room temperature, then refrigerate for at least 4 hours before serving.
8. For brittle
9. Dry the inner pot and to Sauté for 5 mins. Add sugar and water, allow to bubble and heat until golden brown. Push cancel. Carefully pour mixture (it will be very hot!) on to a tray with baking paper and allow to set at room temperature.
10. For caramel
11. Set to Sauté for 7 minutes, push Sauté again until it says Less. Add the sugar and butter and keep stirring slowly until they have melted and dissolved. Slowly pour in the cream and whisk to allow the mixture to thicken. Then remove and set aside for serving.
12. Apple Chips
13. Place the Air Fry basket with tray inserted, into the inner pot. Secure the Air Fry lid and set to Air Fry at 180c. Once hot, open lid and place add cinnamon spiced apple slices to basket.
14. Air Fry for 10 minutes, turning at least twice while grilling.

Vortex Air Fryer Tik Tok Blueberry Cookies

Servings: 12

Cooking Time: 10 Minutes

Ingredients:

- 1 cup flour
- ½ teaspoon baking powder
- ⅛ teaspoon salt
- ⅓ cup vegan butter softened
- ⅓ cup sugar + 1 tablespoon
- ⅓ cup frozen blueberries
- ½ cup white chocolate chips or shavings

Directions:

1. In a small bowl whisk together flour, baking powder, and salt - set aside
2. Thaw blueberries in microwave for about 1 minute until berries are soft and jam like - let cool
3. Cream butter and sugar until light and fluffy
4. Add in blueberries and mix on high until fully incorporated
5. Fold in dry ingredients gradually
6. Mix in white chocolate
7. Chill dough in the freezer for about 30 minutes. Preheat air fryer to 375°F on BAKE.
8. Shape into 12 equal size balls and place in air fryer basket.
9. Bake for 10 minutes, repeat with remaining cookie dough.
10. Let cool, serve, and enjoy!

Grilled Peaches With Burrata

Ingredients:

- 3-4 peaches, sliced
- 1 cup Burrata cheese
- ½ cup balsamic vinegar
- 2 tbsp olive oil
- salt and pepper to taste
- fresh basil
- 2 cups arugula
- sliced baguette

Directions:

1. Pour 2 cups of water into your GoWISE USA Smokeless Grill drip tray. Set your grill to medium high and turn on the fan. Then, brush the sliced peaches with olive oil and grill on medium high for 6 minutes, flipping occasionally.
2. While the peaches are grilling, prepare the balsamic reduction. In a small saucepan, cook the balsamic vinegar over low heat until the vinegar has reduced to at least half the original amount.
3. Slice your baguette and place the sliced pieces on your grill. Brush them with olive oil and grill for 2 minutes on each side.
4. Add grilled peaches to a bed of arugula. Top with Burrata cheese and fresh basil and drizzle on the balsamic reduction. Season with salt and pepper to taste. Serve with toasted baguette slices and enjoy!

Air Fryer Lava Cake

Servings: 2

Cooking Time: 10 Minutes

Ingredients:

- 3 ounces chocolate pieces
- 4 Tablespoons unsalted butter
- 2 large eggs
- 1 large egg white
- 1/3 cup granulated sugar
- 1/4 cup all-purpose flour
- 1 teaspoon confectioner's sugar

Directions:

1. Prepare two 6-ounce ramekins with nonstick cooking spray and set aside.
2. Combine the butter and chocolate in a medium microwave-safe bowl.
3. Melt the chocolate and butter for 60-90 seconds, stirring in 30-second intervals until they are fully melted and combined.
4. In a separate bowl whisk the egg white, eggs, and sugar until the mixture becomes frothy.
5. Carefully pour the egg mixture and sugar mixture into the butter and chocolate mixture and mix them together.
6. Use a spatula and combine the flour with the chocolate batter. Mix until just combined. Do not overmix.
7. Pour the batter into the prepared ramekins.
8. Air fry the molten lava cakes at 370 degrees F for 8-10 minutes. Keep a close eye on them during the cooking process so they don't overcook.

9. Cook until the tops of the lava cakes have popped up and have crispy edges.
10. Allow the ramekins to cool for a minute, then use a thick dish towel and carefully remove them from the air fryer basket.
11. Use a sharp knife to run between the edge of the cake and the ramekins.
12. Carefully flip the cakes onto a serving plate.

Notes

A dusting of confectioners' sugar, colored or chocolate sprinkles, chocolate cream, vanilla ice cream, fresh berries with chocolate shavings, peppermint candies or chocolate sauce.

Use silicone baking cups if you do not have oven-safe ramekins. Do not use an electric beater or electric mixer, this will take the air out of the batter so the molten lava cakes will not be airy and have a liquid chocolate center.

Use a butter knife or a flat spatula that you use for icing a cake if you do not want to use a sharp knife.

I make this recipe in my Cosori 5.8 qt. air fryer. Depending on your air fryer, size and wattages, cook time may need to be adjusted a couple of minutes.

Air Fryer Apple Fritters

Servings: 12

Cooking Time: 6 Minutes

Ingredients:

- 2 apples, cored and diced
- 1 cup all-purpose flour
- 2 tablespoons sugar
- 1 teaspoon baking powder
- 1/2 teaspoon salt
- 1/2 teaspoon ground cinnamon
- 1/4 teaspoon ground nutmeg
- 1/3 cup milk
- 2 tablespoons butter, melted
- 1 egg
- 1/2 teaspoon lemon juice
- CINNAMON GLAZE
- 1/2 cup confectioners sugar
- 2 tablespoons milk
- 1/2 teaspoon ground cinnamon
- Pinch of salt

Directions:

1. Dice the apples into small cubes and set aside. Peel them if desired.
2. Add the flour, sugar, baking powder, salt, ground cinnamon, and ground nutmeg into a large mixing bowl and stir to combine.
3. In a separate bowl, mix the milk, butter,* egg, and lemon juice.
4. Add the wet ingredients into the dry ingredients and stir just until combined. Stir in the apples and put mixture into the fridge for anywhere from 5 minutes to 2 days (covered).
5. Preheat your air fryer to 370 degrees.
6. Put a parchment round on the bottom of the basket and scoop out apple fritters into 2-tablespoon balls. Place apple fritters in the air fryer and cook for 6-7 minutes.
7. While cooking, whisk the confectioners sugar, milk, cinnamon, and salt together to make the glaze.
8. Remove the apple fritters from the air fryer, place them on a wire rack, and immediately pour the glaze over top and enjoy!

Notes

*to make the apple fritters even fluffier, grate the butter in cold to the recipe instead of using melted butter.

HOW TO REHEAT APPLE FRITTERS IN THE AIR FRYER:

Preheat your air fryer to 320 degrees.

Cook apple fritters for 2-3 minutes and enjoy! If cooking from refrigerated, add 1-2 additional minutes.

Air Fryer Brie

Servings: 4

Cooking Time: 5 Minutes

Ingredients:

- 8 ounces Brie Cheese
- 2 tablespoons dried cranberries or cherries
- 2 tablespoons sliced almonds
- 1 tablespoon honey or flavored liqueur such as Chambord or Bailey's Irish Creme
- 1 small baguette sliced and toasted

Directions:

1. Prepare the cheese by removing the brie rind on top of the cheese wheel only. Leave the rind around the sides and bottom of the cheese.
2. Place cheese in a small ramekin or oven safe dish. Place brie in center or your basket. Air fry at 350 degrees F for 5-7 minutes until the cheese is soft and warm.
3. While cheese is in air fryer, in a small, microwave safe bowl, combine the cranberries, almonds, and honey or liquor. Stir together and then microwave for 30-45 seconds, until warm.
4. Pour ingredients over the top of the brie and serve while hot.

Notes

Optional Flavors: spiced rum, fig jam, Cointreau, maple syrup, kalua, or berry cranberry sauce.

Optional Toppings: cranberry sauce, roasted mushrooms, drizzle of dark chocolate, tangy brie honey mixture, an artichoke-sundried tomato mixture, caramel sauce, crumbled air fryer bacon, air fryer candied chopped walnuts or pistachios.

Cooking Tips: Use a sharp knife to cut away rind on top of cheese so you keep as much cheese on the wheel to enjoy later.

Air Fryer Chocolate Chip-cream Cheese-stuffed Cinnamon Rolls

Servings: 8

Ingredients:

- 4 oz (from 8-oz package) cream cheese, softened
- 1/4 cup powdered sugar
- 3 tablespoons miniature semisweet chocolate chips
- 1 can (12.4 oz) refrigerated Pillsbury™ Cinnamon Rolls with Original Icing (8 Count)

Directions:

1. Cut 8-inch round of cooking parchment paper. Place in bottom of air fryer basket.
2. In small bowl, stir cream cheese, powdered sugar and chocolate chips until combined.
3. Separate dough into 8 rolls; place cinnamon side up. Press each roll into 4-inch round. Spoon 1 heaping tablespoonful of the cream cheese mixture into center of each round. Gently fold edges up and over filling; pinch to seal. Place 4 cinnamon rolls on parchment in air fryer basket, seam sides down, spacing apart.
4. Set air fryer to 325°F; cook 7 to 8 minutes or until cinnamon roll tops are light brown. With tongs, turn over each one; cook 5 to 6 minutes or until golden brown and cooked through. Remove from air fryer. Repeat with remaining cinnamon rolls.
5. Transfer icing to small microwavable bowl. Microwave uncovered on Low (10%) 8 to 10 seconds or until thin enough to drizzle. Place rolls on serving plate; use a spoon to drizzle icing over rolls. Serve warm.

Air-fried Raspberry Brie Bites

Servings: 16

Cooking Time: 15 Minutes

Ingredients:

- 1 (8 ounce) round Brie cheese
- 1 (8 ounce) package phyllo dough, thawed
- 1 cup raspberry jam
- 1 cup butter, melted
- 2 tablespoons honey
- flakey salt to taste

Directions:

1. Slice the brie into squares about ½ inch thick and 1 to 1 ½ inches wide.
2. Roll out 1 sheet of phyllo dough vertically on a large work surface. Brush the bottom half of the dough with melted butter, then fold the top half over onto itself.
3. Place 1 piece of cheese in the bottom center of the dough, about 2 inches from the edges. Spoon about 2 teaspoons raspberry jam onto the cheese. Brush melted butter around the rest of the dough.
4. Fold in the bottom 2 inches of dough over the cheese, then fold in both sides. Brush more butter onto the remaining dough, then carefully roll the filling upwards until it is wrapped fully. Brush more butter on top and set into the air fryer try.
5. Set air fryer to 375 degrees F (190 degrees C).
6. Air fry in batches to avoid overcrowding until golden-brown, 4 to 5 minutes. Garnish with a thin drizzle of honey and a pinch of flakey salt. Serve immediately.

Air Fryer Smuckers Uncrustables

Servings: 4

Cooking Time: 8 Minutes

Ingredients:

- 2 to 4 Frozen Uncrustables
- 2 tablespoons butter, melted (optional)

Directions:

1. Brush the tops of your frozen Uncrustables with your melted butter (optional), to make the Uncrustables a little less dry.
2. Place them in your air fryer basket leaving space around them for the air to circulate. Turn your fryer to 350 and cook for 6-8 minutes, flipping them halfway through cooking.
3. Remove the Uncrustables from the air fryer and enjoy!

Notes

Brushing just the tops with butter gives it the golden crunchy side. The bottom remains soft but it is a perfect combination with the gooey center.

Chai Doughnuts

Servings: 8-10

Cooking Time: 5 Minutes

Ingredients:

- 2 c flour
- 3 tsp of Sweetly (or sweetener of your liking)
- 10g active dry yeast
- 1 tbsp Vegan Flora Spread (or other vegan butter)
- 1 tsp Chai Essence
- ½ c water
- ½ c soy milk

Directions:

1. Warm your soy milk slightly. Add your sweetener and mix until it is dissolved. Then add your active dry yeast, mix and set it aside for 10 minutes.
2. Add your flour, water and butter and combine until you have a smooth ball of dough. Cover the bowl with a cloth and set aside to rest for a minimum of 2 hours. You can also proof your dough in the Instant Pot, see here.
3. The dough should have doubled in size. Prepare your cooking area by putting down some. You can use a glass bottle if you don't own a rolling pin and

roll the dough to be about 3cm thick. Using a greased doughnut cutter, cut them into shapes.

4. Lightly grease the Duo Crisp tray and pack your doughnuts. Cover using your Air Fryer Lid and bake at 180 degrees Celsius for 5 minutes.

5. For the cinnamon-sugar coating, all you need is to brush your doughnuts with some soy milk to make it stick. We made a mixture of Sweetly and cinnamon to cut down on the sugar, as well as the calories for a healthier alternative.

6. Enjoy!

Air Fryer Baked Apples

Servings: 4

Cooking Time: 8 Minutes

Ingredients:
- 4 medium apples
- 2 tablespoons oats
- 2 tablespoons raisins
- 2 tablespoons walnuts chopped
- 1 tablespoon brown sugar
- 1/2 teaspoon cinnamon
- 1 tablespoon butter melted

Directions:
1. In a medium bowl, combine the oats, raisins, brown sugar, walnuts, and cinnamon. Stir in the melted butter until the ingredients are combined. Set the bowl aside to prepare the apples.

2. Cut the tops of the apple off along with the stem. Then, cut a small part of the bottom of the apple as well, so it stands up without shifting or rolling.

3. Use an apple corer, melon baller or paring knife to scoop out the apple core and remove all seeds. Spoon the mixture into the cored apples until they are filled. Place the filled apples into the air fryer basket.

4. Air fry apples at 350 degrees Fahrenheit for 8 to 10 minutes until the apples reach your desired softness. Let apples cool just enough to remove from basket, and serve warm.

Notes

Don't remove to much of the apple cavity, just make a small hollow center to fill with the oat mixture, about ¾ of inch wide.

Be careful to not go all the way to the bottom of the apple or the crumble filling may fall through the bottom of apple while air frying.

When you select apples for this recipe, I use medium size apples. Depending on size of apples, you may need to adjust cook time. The larger apples work best to add filling.

Air Fryer Banana Muffins

Servings: 18

Cooking Time: 20 Minutes

Ingredients:
- 2 ripe bananas
- 150g (1 cup) self-raising flour
- 60g (1/3 cup, lightly packed) brown sugar
- 1 egg
- 60ml (1/4 cup) olive oil
- 60ml (1/4 cup) buttermilk
- Maple syrup, to brush, plus extra (optional), to serve
- Select all Ingredients:

Directions:
1. Use a fork to mash the bananas in a small bowl. Set aside until required.

2. Use a balloon whisk to whisk the flour and sugar in a medium bowl. Make a well in the centre. Add the egg, oil and buttermilk. Use the whisk to break up the egg. Use a wooden spoon to stir until the mixture is combined. Stir through the banana.

3. Preheat an air fryer to 180C. Divide half of the mixture among 9 patty cases. Remove the rack from the air fryer and carefully transfer the cases to the rack. Return the rack to the fryer. Cook for 8-10 minutes or until muffins are cooked through. Transfer to a wire rack. Repeat with the remaining mixture to make 18 muffins.

4. Brush the tops of the muffins with maple syrup while still warm. Serve with extra maple syrup, if you like.

Notes

You'll need 18 paper patty cases for this recipe. Store the muffins in an airtight container for up to 3 days.

Air-fryer Lemon Slice Sugar Cookies

Servings: 2

Cooking Time: 10 Minutes

Ingredients:

- 1/2 cup unsalted butter, softened
- 1 package (3.4 ounces) instant lemon pudding mix
- 1/2 cup sugar
- 1 large egg, room temperature
- 2 tablespoons 2% milk
- 1-1/2 cups all-purpose flour
- 1 teaspoon baking powder
- 1/4 teaspoon salt
- ICING:
- 2/3 cup confectioners' sugar
- 2 to 4 teaspoons lemon juice

Directions:

1. In a large bowl, cream butter, pudding mix and sugar until light and fluffy, 5-7 minutes. Beat in egg and milk. In another bowl, whisk flour, baking powder and salt; gradually beat into creamed mixture.
2. Divide dough in half. On a lightly floured surface, shape each into a 6-in.-long roll. Wrap and refrigerate 3 hours or until firm.
3. Preheat air fryer to 325°. Unwrap and cut dough crosswise into 1/2-in. slices. In batches, place slices in a single layer on a parchment-lined air-fryer basket. Cook until edges are light brown, 8-12 minutes. Cool in basket 2 minutes. Remove to wire racks to cool completely.
4. In a small bowl, mix confectioners' sugar and enough lemon juice to reach a drizzling consistency. Drizzle over cookies. Let stand until set.
5. To Make Ahead: Dough can be made 2 days in advance. Wrap and place in a resealable container. Store in the refrigerator.

Air Fryer Heart Shaped Whoopie Pies

Ingredients:

- 1 package of strawberry or red velvet cake mix
- 3 large eggs
- ½ cup canola oil
- 1/2 cup water
- 2 tsp vanilla extract
- 8 oz cream cheese
- ½ cup butter, softened
- 2 cups confectioners' sugar
- 1 cup miniature semisweet chocolate chips

Directions:

1. In a large bowl, combine cake mix, eggs, oil, and vanilla extract. Stir until combined.
2. Fill greased ramekins ¾ of the way full with batter.
3. Bake at 350°F for 25 minutes. Allow cakes to cool before removing them from ramekins.
4. For filling, beat cream cheese and butter together in a large bowl until blended. Gradually beat in confectioners' sugar until smooth. Stir in chocolate chips.
5. Cut the top layers off the cakes. Cut the remaining cake in half and fill with filling mixture. Decorate the tops as desired – we used a heart shaped cookie cutter and some sprinkles. Enjoy!

Air Fryer Apple Cider Biscuit Doughnuts

Servings: 8

Ingredients:

- 1 cup powdered sugar
- 2 tablespoons apple cider
- 1/4 teaspoon apple pie spice or ground cinnamon
- 6 tablespoons butter, melted
- 1 can (16.3 oz) refrigerated Pillsbury™ Grands!™ Southern Homestyle Original Biscuits (8 Count)

Directions:

1. In medium bowl, beat powdered sugar, apple cider, apple pie spice and 2 tablespoons of the butter with whisk. Set aside for glaze.
2. Spray bottom of air fryer basket with cooking spray. Separate dough into 8 biscuits. Place biscuits on cutting board. With 1-inch round cookie cutter, cut hole in center of each biscuit.
3. Place remaining 4 tablespoons butter in medium bowl. Dip all sides of biscuits and centers into butter; shake off excess butter. Place 4 biscuits in air fryer basket, spacing apart.
4. Set air fryer to 370°F; cook 3 to 6 minutes or until biscuit tops are deep golden brown. Using tongs or spatula, turn over each biscuit. Cook 1 to 4 minutes or until deep golden brown and cooked through. Remove from air fryer; cover loosely with foil to keep warm while cooking second batch. Cook as directed above for remaining 4 biscuits. Remove from air fryer; cover loosely with foil to keep warm while cooking centers.
5. Place 8 biscuit centers in bottom of air fryer basket. Set air fryer to 370°F; cook 2 minutes. Using tongs or spatula, turn over each biscuit center. Cook 1 to 3 minutes or until deep golden brown and cooked through.
6. Turn each doughnut upside down, and dip halfway into glaze. Let any excess drip off, then transfer right side up to cooling rack or serving plate. Serve warm.

Air Fryer Caramilk Crumpet French Toast

Servings: 3

Cooking Time: 15 Minutes

Ingredients:

- 100g Caramilk chocolate, grated, plus extra to serve
- 6g salted butter, softened
- 6 round crumpets
- 2 eggs
- 1 tbsp milk
- 1/2 cup sweetened condensed milk
- Thickened cream, whipped
- Select all Ingredients:

Directions:

1. Line the base of an air fryer with foil, ensuring it comes at least 1 inch up the sides of the basket.
2. Combine Caramilk and butter in a bowl. Divide into 6 portions. Spread each portion over each crumpet. Cut each crumpet in half and sandwich together.
3. Whisk eggs with milk and 2 tbsp of sweetened condensed milk. Dip each crumpet sandwich in the egg mixture, coating well on all sides. Place in the air fryer basket. Repeat with remaining crumpet sandwiches. Pour over remaining sweetened condensed milk. Cook at 150C for 15 minutes or until crumpets are golden and caramelised.
4. To serve, grate over extra Caramilk and top with whipped cream.

Air Fryer Cheese Curds

Servings: 8

Cooking Time: 15 Minutes

Ingredients:

- 12 ounces cheese curds, cut into 1 1/2 inch pieces.
- 1 1/2 cups panko bread crumbs
- 3 eggs
- 1/4 cup all purpose flour
- 1/2 cup grated Parmesan cheese
- 1 tablespoon minced fresh parsley
- 1/2 teaspoon Italian seasoning
- 1/2 teaspoon salt
- 1/4 teaspoon pepper

Directions:

1. In a small bowl, combine panko bread crumbs, Parmesan, Italian seasoning, parsley, salt and pepper.
2. Whisk the eggs in a second bowl and add the flour to a third bowl.
3. Dip each cheese curd into the flour, then the egg, then the bread crumb mixture. Be sure it is fully coated each time.
4. Dip the coated cheese curd back into the egg, then into the bread crumb mixture again.
5. Spray air fryer basket with olive oil using an oil mister (**do NOT use aerosol cooking spray, as it can damage the inside of the basket**).
6. Place cheese curds in air fryer basket, being careful not to overcrowd, and air fry at 400° for 6-8 minutes, flipping halfway through. Watch carefully to make sure they don't overcook!
7. Repeat as necessary until all cheese curds are done.

Air Fryer Gf Peanut Butter Chocolate Chip Cookies

Servings: 2

Ingredients:

- 1 large egg
- 1 c. creamy peanut butter
- 1/3 c. packed light brown sugar
- 1 tsp. pure vanilla extract
- 1/2 tsp. baking soda
- Pinch of kosher salt
- 1/3 c. semisweet chocolate chips

Directions:

1. In a medium bowl, whisk egg until well beaten. Add peanut butter, brown sugar, vanilla, baking soda, and salt. Stir until combined and mixture thickens a bit, about 15 seconds. Fold in chips.
2. Roll dough into 1" balls (about 1 level tablespoon each). Flatten each ball to a disk about 1 1/2" wide. Transfer to a plate.
3. Line an air-fryer basket with foil, leaving a 1" to 2" overhang on 2 opposite sides. Working in batches, arrange cookies in basket, spacing about 1/2" apart. Cook at 350° until deeply browned, 5 to 7 minutes. Carefully, as foil will be hot, remove foil with cookies from air-fryer basket. Transfer to a wire rack and let cool on foil until cookies firm up, about 5 minutes. Using a thin spatula, transfer cookies to wire rack and let cool completely.

POULTRY RECIPES

Chicken Fajitas With Spicy Potatoes

Servings: 4

Ingredients:
- 3 chicken breats
- 1 tbsp smoked paprika
- 1 tbsp ground coriander
- 1 tsp ground cumin
- 1 tsp garlic powder
- 1/2 tsp dried chilli flakes
- 1 tsp dried oregano
- 4 tbsp olive oil
- 1 juice of lime
- salt and freshly ground black pepper
- 1 onion, peeled and sliced
- 1 red pepper, de-seeded and sliced
- 1 yellow pepper, de-seeded and sliced
- 8 medium tortillas
- For the spicy potatoes
- 1kg baby potatoes, cut in quarters
- 3 tbsp olive oil
- 2 tsp hot paprika
- 1 tbsp garlic powder
- 1 tbsp smoked paprika
- 1 tsp sea salt
- COOKING MODE
- When entering cooking mode - We will enable your screen to stay 'always on' to avoid any unnecessary interruptions whilst you cook!

Directions:
1. Slice chicken breasts into thin strips.
2. Add spices, herbs, lime juice and oil into a large bowl, season to taste and mix together.
3. Stir in chicken pieces, onion and peppers, mix all together until everything is coated in the marinade.
4. In another bowl, toss potatoes in oil and spices
5. Insert a crisper plate in both drawers. Add chicken and vegetables to zone 1 drawer and potatoes to zone 2 drawer and insert into unit.
6. Select zone 1, select AIR FRY, set temperature to 200°C and set time to 20 minutes. Select zone 2 and select ROAST, set temperature to 180°C and set time to 25 minutes. Select SYNC. Select START/STOP to begin.
7. After 10 minutes, give both drawers a shake or stir. Repeat again after 15 minutes.
8. When zone 1 time reaches 0, check chicken is cooked. Cooking is complete when the internal temperature reaches at least 75°C on an instant read thermometer.
9. Serve chicken and vegetables wrapped in the tortillas with the potatoes on the side.

How To Make Juicy Air Fryer Chicken Breasts

Servings: 4

Cooking Time: 10 Minutes

Ingredients:
- kosher salt* (see notes)
- 4 boneless chicken breasts (about 6 ounces each)
- olive oil spray
- 3/4 teaspoon garlic powder
- 3/4 teaspoon onion powder
- 1/2 teaspoon dried parsley
- 1/2 teaspoon smoked paprika
- 1/8 cayenne pepper

Directions:
1. Air Fryer Directions:
2. Pound the thicker end of the chicken to make both sides leveled out so they cook evenly.
3. Fill a large bowl with 6 cups of lukewarm water and add 1/4 cup Diamond Crystal kosher salt, stir to dissolve.
4. Add the chicken breasts to the water and let them sit, refrigerated 1 to 1 1/2 hours to brine. Remove from water, pat dry with paper towels and discard the water.
5. In a small bowl combine 3/4 teaspoon salt, with the remaining spices. Spritz the chicken with oil and rub all over, then rub the spice mix over the chicken.
6. Add the chicken to the air fryer basket and air fry in batches 380F 5 minutes on each side, 10 minutes total until browned on the outside and cooked

through on the inside. See notes below for larger breasts.

7. Oven Directions:
8. Preheat the oven to 350F. Heat an oven safe or cast iron skillet over high heat for 5 minutes until it is very hot.
9. Place the chicken on the hot skillet, and cook for 1 minute. Turn, and cook 1 minute on other side.
10. Transfer skillet to the oven and bake until no longer pink in the center and the juices run clear and a thermometer reads 165F inserted in the center, about 8 to 10 minutes.

Notes

How Long To Cook Chicken Breast in the Air Fryer
The amount of time it takes to cook chicken in an air fryer will vary based on the thickness and size of your chicken breasts. The internal temp for cooked chicken breast should be 165 degrees F.
Small Breasts (5 to 6 ounces): 8 to 10 minutes
Medium Breasts (7 to 8 ounces): 10 to 12 minutes
Large Breasts (9 ounces or more): 12 to 14 minutes
Always flip the chicken breast halfway through cooking to ensure it cooks evenly.
*Be sure your salt is Kosher in this brine. I use Diamond Crystal kosher salt which has half the sodium are Mortons. Table salt will be too salty.

Air Fryer Crispy Coconut Chicken Tenders

Servings: 4

Cooking Time: 12 Minutes

Ingredients:

- 1.5 lbs. boneless skinless chicken breasts ~3 chicken breasts
- 1 cup unsweetened shredded coconut
- 1 tablespoon garlic powder
- ½ cup plain breadcrumbs
- 1 teaspoon chili powder
- 1 teaspoon salt
- 2 large eggs
- 2 tablespoons melted coconut oil separated

Directions:

1. Preheat the air fryer to 380°F and drizzle 2 teaspoons of coconut oil into the air fryer or spray with coconut oil cooking spray.
2. Slice the chicken breasts into 2-inch wide by 4-inch long strips. Set aside.
3. Add the coconut, garlic powder, breadcrumbs, chili powder, and salt to a medium bowl and mix until combined.
4. In a separate bowl add 2 large eggs to a bowl and whisk.
5. Dredge the chicken strips through the egg mixture and then dredge the chicken strips in the coconut mixture, making sure the strips are fully coated.
6. Place the chicken strips into the air fryer basket, making sure they are not overlapping or overcrowded. You will have to cook these chicken strips in two or three batches depending on the size of your air fryer.
7. Drizzle the chicken with 1-2 teaspoons of melted coconut oil. Then, air fry the chicken strips for 6 minutes, flip, and cook for an additional 5 minutes or until the internal temperature reaches 165°F.
8. Remove the chicken from the air fryer and repeat until all the chicken strips are cooked.
9. Serve with your favorite sauces

Tips & Notes

We do not recommend using sweetened coconut.
Everybody's air fryer is different, so monitor your chicken while it is cooking to be sure it doesn't overcook.

Air Fryer Chicken Wings With Dry Rub

Servings: 4-6

Cooking Time: 20 Minutes

Ingredients:

- 3 pounds chicken wings
- 2 tablespoons baking powder
- 2 teaspoons paprika
- 2 teaspoons garlic powder
- 1 ½ teaspoons dried oregano
- 1 teaspoon dried thyme
- 1 teaspoon onion powder
- 1 teaspoon cayenne pepper
- 1 teaspoon kosher salt
- 1 teaspoon black pepper
- ¼ teaspoon red pepper flakes (optional)

Directions:

1. Pat the wings dry and place them in a large bowl or plastic bag.
2. Sprinkle the baking powder and spices over the chicken, tossing until they're fully coated.
3. Working in batches, place the wings in a single layer in the air fryer basket. Lightly spray the chicken with cooking oil spray.
4. Air fry at 400 degrees F for 15 minutes. Flip the wings, spray them with cooking oil, and air fry for an additional 5 minutes, or until the chicken is crispy and cooked through to 165 degrees F internally.

Notes

To Make Frozen Chicken Wings, Start By Cooking Them For 5 Minutes At 400 Degrees F To Defrost Them, Then Follow The Full Recipe Like Usual.

Air Fryer Chicken Wings

Servings: 4

Cooking Time: 35 Minutes

Ingredients:

- 2 lb Chicken wings (flats and drumettes, either fresh or thawed from frozen)
- 1 tbsp Olive oil (optional)
- 2 tsp Baking powder
- 3/4 tsp Sea salt
- 1/4 tsp Black pepper

Directions:

1. Pat the chicken wings very dry with paper towels. (This will help them get crispy.)
2. In a large bowl, toss the wings with baking powder, olive oil (if using), sea salt and black pepper.
3. Place the chicken wings in the air fryer in a single layer, without touching too much. (Cook in batches if they don't fit.)
4. Air fry the chicken wings for 15 minutes at 250 degrees F. (If your wings are frozen, add an extra 10 minutes at this step.)
5. Flip the wings over. Increase the air fryer temperature to 430 degrees F (or the highest your air fryer goes). Air fry for about 15 to 20 minutes, until chicken wings are done and crispy.

Air Fryer Whole Chicken

Servings: 6

Cooking Time: 44 Minutes

Ingredients:

- 3 lb whole chicken
- 2 tablespoons olive oil
- 1/2 teaspoon salt
- 1/2 teaspoon pepper
- 1 teaspoon smoked paprika
- 1 teaspoon Italian seasonings
- 1/4 teaspoon Rosemary
- 1/4 teaspoon mustard powder

Directions:

1. Preheat the air fryer to 180C/350F.
2. Pat dry the chicken, then drizzle the olive oil on all sides.
3. In a small bowl, combine all the spices. Rub the spices all over the chicken.
4. Place the chicken in the air fryer breast side down. Air fry for 25 minutes before flipping and cooking for a further 20 minutes. Once the chicken reaches an internal temperature of 165F, remove it from the air fryer.
5. Let the chicken rest for 5 minutes before carving.

Notes

TO STORE: Place leftover chicken in an airtight container and store it in the refrigerator for up to 5 days.

TO FREEZE: Once the chicken has cooled to room temperature, place in a ziplock bag and store it in the freezer for up to 3 months. You can also shred it before doing so.

TO REHEAT: Microwave portions of the chicken for 20-30 seconds or reheat in a preheated oven until warm.

Air Fryer Cheddar Ranch Chicken Tenders

Servings: 8

Ingredients:

- 2 tablespoons all-purpose flour
- 2 teaspoons Montreal chicken seasoning
- 1/3 cup ranch dressing
- 2/3 cup Progresso™ plain panko crispy bread crumbs
- 1/2 cup finely shredded sharp cheddar cheese (2 oz)
- 1 package (14 oz) boneless skinless chicken tenders

Directions:

1. Cut 8-inch round of cooking parchment paper. Place in bottom of air fryer basket. Spray with cooking spray.
2. In shallow dish, mix flour and seasoning. In another shallow dish, place ranch dressing. In third shallow dish, mix bread crumbs and cheddar cheese. Coat chicken with flour mixture; dip into ranch dressing, then coat with bread crumb mixture, pressing to adhere.
3. Place chicken on parchment in air fryer basket, standing chicken against sides of basket, if necessary. Set to 325°F; cook 10 minutes. Turn chicken; cook 10 to 15 minutes longer or until chicken is no longer pink in center.

Air Fryer Popcorn Chicken

Servings: 4

Cooking Time: 10 Minutes

Ingredients:

- 1 tablespoon olive oil
- 1 ½ cup panko breadcrumbs*
- 1 teaspoon kosher salt (divided)
- 1 pound boneless (skinless chicken breasts)
- 2 tablespoons all-purpose flour
- 1 large egg
- 2 teaspoons garlic powder
- 2 teaspoons onion powder
- 1 teaspoon dried oregano
- 1/8 teaspoon cayenne pepper (optional)
- Freshly ground black pepper
- Olive oil spray
- Ketchup, Low Fat Ranch Dressing, BBQ Sauce, Honey Mustard, Marinara (Optional, for dipping)

Directions:

1. Add oil to a medium skillet over medium low heat. Add the panko and ½ teaspoon salt.
2. Toast panko for about 4 minutes or until just golden, stirring every 30 seconds to evenly brown. Transfer crumbs to a plate.
3. Cut chicken into ¾-inch cubes (about the size of a small dice), season with ¼ teaspoon salt and pepper, to taste, then set up your dredging station. You should have about 60 cubes.
4. To set up dredging station:
5. Place flour and ¼ teaspoon salt on a large plate.
6. Place egg in a bowl, add 1 teaspoon water and beat until uniform.
7. Add the garlic powder, onion powder, oregano and cayenne (if using) and black pepper, to taste, to the toasted panko and place the plate on the other side of the egg bowl.
8. Working with about 15 pieces at a time, dredge in flour, lightly coating all sides.
9. Then, egg, allowing excess to drip off (I like to use tongs and wipe the excess off on the side of the bowl). Next add the pieces to the panko mixture and coat all sides evenly, pressing crumbs to make sure they adhere evenly. Repeat with remaining pieces.
10. Preheat air fryer to 400 degrees F. Spray the basket with olive oil.
11. Add about 30 pieces to the air fryer basket, making sure to leave space between each piece so they get crispy. Spray the top with oil.
12. Cook for 5 minutes, shaking the basket halfway through cook time. Serve immediately.

Notes

*1/4 cup breadcrumbs get thrown out

For best results, freeze Popcorn Chicken UNCOOKED.

Place chicken pieces in an even layer (not stacked top of each other) in a freezer safe container lined with parchment, adding a new piece of parchment to each layer.

When ready to cook, heat the air fryer to 400 degrees F. Spray the basket with oil then add 30 pieces, in an even layer. Cook for 8 minutes, shaking the basket halfway through cook time.

Air Fryer Orange Chicken

Ingredients:

- For Sauce:
- ½ Tbsp. soy sauce
- 5 Tbsp. sugar
- 5 Tbsp. white vinegar
- Orange zest, grated
- Chicken
- ½ cup + 1 Tbsp. cornstarch
- ¼ cup flour
- ¼ cup water
- 1 egg
- 1 ½ tsp salt
- 1 ½ tsp white pepper
- 1 Tbsp. ginger root, minced
- 1 tsp garlic, minced
- ¼ cup green onions, chopped
- ½ tsp crushed red pepper
- 1 Tbsp. Shaoxing rice wine
- 2 Tbsp. sesame oil
- 2 lbs. chicken breasts, boneless & skinless

Directions:

1. In a medium mixing bowl, combine the soy sauce, white vinegar, sugar and orange zest to make the sauce, mix well; Set aside.
2. Add in the flour and the ½ cup cornstarch in another bowl and stir together.
3. In another separate bowl, add in the egg, white pepper, salt, and the 1 Tbsp of sesame oil and whisk until combined.
4. Slice the chicken into about 1 inch pieces. Dip each piece into the egg mixture, then the flour mixture until fully coated. Fully dust off any excess flour.
5. Line the air fryer basket with perforated parchment paper (optional) and place the chicken pieces in the air fryer- or utilize your dehydrating racks like we did! Air fry at 400°F for 4 minutes. Once finished, switch the positioning of your racks and air fry at 400°F for another 4 minutes. We recommend spraying with Olive Oil spray to ensure a crispy result.

Breaded Chicken Cutlets With Deconstructed Guacamole

Servings: 4

Cooking Time: 20 Minutes

Ingredients:

- For The Chicken:
- 2 8 ounce boneless chicken breasts (cut in half lengthwise to make 4 thinner cutlets)
- 1/4 teaspoon seasoned salt (such as adobo seasoning)
- 2 large egg whites (beaten)
- 1/2 teaspoon Sazon (homemade or packaged)
- 1/2 cup seasoned breadcrumbs (or gluten-free crumbs)
- 1 -1/2 tbsp olive oil
- For the Deconstructed Guacamole:
- 4 ounces avocado (from 1 small Hass)
- 1 cup grape tomatoes (halved)
- 1/4 cup slivered red onion
- 1/4 cup cilantro leaves
- 1/4 teaspoon kosher salt and black pepper
- 1/4 teaspoon cumin
- juice of 1/2 lime
- 4 lime wedges for serving

Directions:

1. Season cutlets with seasoned salt. Place bread crumbs in a shallow bowl. In another bowl beat egg whites sazon together. Dip chicken cutlets in egg whites, then breadcrumb mixture, shaking off excess.
2. Heat a large nonstick frying pan on medium heat. Add the olive oil. When hot add the cutlets and cook about 6 minutes on each side, until golden brown and cooked through.
3. In a large bowl combine the avocado, red onion, tomato, cilantro, salt, pepper, cumin, and lime juice. Gently toss and serve over the chicken with additional lime wedges.
4. Air Fryer Directions:
5. Air fry in batches 400F 6 to 7 minutes turning halfway, until the crumbs are golden brown and the center is no longer pink.

Air Fryer Chicken Thighs

Servings: 4

Cooking Time: 20 Minutes

Ingredients:

- 4-5 chicken thighs bone in, skin on
- 1 tbsp olive oil
- 1 tsp ground black pepper
- 1 tsp onion powder
- 1 tsp garlic powder

Directions:

1. Preheat the air fryer to 400 degrees Fahrenheit.
2. Rinse and pat the chicken thighs dry with a paper towel. Place the chicken in a small bowl and toss in the olive oil.
3. Add the seasonings to the chicken thighs and make sure to cover them evenly.
4. Place the thighs into the air fryer basket in a single layer.
5. Air Fry at 400 degrees Fahrenheit for 15 minutes of cooking time. Flip the chicken thighs and cook for an additional 8 minutes.
6. Use a meat thermometer to ensure the thighs have reached an internal temperature of 165 degrees Fahrenheit.
7. For a crispier skin, cook for an additional 1-2 minutes before serving.

Notes

Serve this recipe with baked potatoes, biscuits, and gravy. Or, for a healthier meal, choose to serve them with a simple side salad with light dressing.

Weight Watchers 4 points

KETO C/2 P/19 F/22

Air Fryer Lemon Pepper Wings

Servings: 4

Cooking Time: 33 Minutes

Ingredients:

- 1 pound chicken wings
- 1 tablespoon olive oil
- 1 ½ tablespoons butter melted
- 1 ½ teaspoons lemon pepper seasoning

Directions:

1. Preheat air fryer to 400°F.
2. Dry wings and coat with olive oil and in a large bowl.
3. Place wings in a single layer in the basket and cook for 22 minutes flipping the wings after 10 minutes.
4. While the wings are cooking melt butter and combine in a bowl with the lemon pepper seasoning.
5. Remove wings from the air fryer and toss with the butter mixture.

Bacon-wrapped Air Fryer Chicken Breasts

Servings: 4

Cooking Time: 18 Minutes

Ingredients:

- 4 skinless boneless chicken breasts (8 ounces each)
- 8 slices center cut bacon
- 1/2 teaspoon kosher salt
- freshly ground black pepper (to taste)

Directions:

1. Season the chicken breasts with salt and black pepper.
2. Starting from one end, tightly wrap two strips of bacon over each chicken breast.
3. Transfer the chicken to the air fryer and air fry 380F about 6 minutes on each side, or until the internal temperature of the chicken has reached 160F then increase to 400F for 1 minute to brown the bacon.
4. Remove from the air fryer and transfer to a cutting board, let rest covered with foil for 5 minutes before slicing.

Notes

No Air Fryer? No Problem

To make this in the oven, preheat the oven to 400F.
Heat a large oven safe or cast-iron skillet over medium-high heat. Sear bacon wrapped chicken breasts on both sides for about 2 minutes per side, or until the bacon is crisp, drain excess fat.

Transfer the chicken to the oven and bake about 12 minutes, or until the internal temperature of the chicken has reached 160F. Remove from the oven and transfer to a cutting board, let rest covered with foil for 5 minutes before slicing.

Air Fryer Stuffed Chicken Breast

Servings: 3

Cooking Time: 15 Minutes

Ingredients:

- 3 boneless, skinless chicken breasts
- salt and pepper to taste
- 4 ounces of cream cheese, softened
- 1 1/2 cup of chopped spinach
- 1/2 cup of mozzarella
- 1/4 cup of parmesan
- 3 tablespoon diced roasted red pepper
- 2 tablespoons of mayo
- 1 1/2 teaspoons minced garlic (1 to 2 cloves)
- 1 1/2 teaspoons paprika
- 1 1/2 teaspoons garlic powder
- 1 1/2 teaspoons onion powder

Directions:

1. Season your chicken with salt and pepper to taste.
2. Combine your filling: cream cheese, mozzarella, parmesan, mayo, garlic, spinach and roasted red peppers.
3. Combine your seasonings: paprika, garlic powder, and onion powder.
4. Filet your chicken breast lengthwise, without cutting all the way through. Lay your chicken breast open and season with ½ to 1 teaspoon of the seasoning. Then spread about ½ cup of the spinach and cheese mixture on one side. Fold your chicken breast over and then piece toothpicks along the seam to try and keep as much spinach and cheese inside as it cooks. Sprinkle the top of your chicken with additional seasoning.

5. Brush olive oil in your air fryer basket, as the nonstick spray is shown to cause your basket to wear faster. Preheat your air fryer at 380 degrees F.
6. Then lay two breasts in at a time, cooking in batches if you cannot fit all Cook for 15 to 18 minutes till a meat thermometer reads 165 degrees F.

Notes

HOW TO REHEAT AIR FRYER STUFFED CHICKEN BREAST:

Preheat your air fryer to 350 degrees.

Place your stuffed chicken in the basket and cook at 350 degrees F for 5 to 8 minutes until warmed.

HOW TO COOK FROZEN STUFFED CHICKEN BREASTS IN THE AIR FRYER:

Preheat your air fryer to 390 degrees.

Heat precooked frozen stuffed chicken breasts in the air fryer for 15 to 17 minutes, until chicken reaches 165 degrees F.

Air Fryer Cheesy Chicken Sausage Rolls

Servings: 24

Cooking Time: 30 Minutes

Ingredients:

- 500g chicken mince
- 125g can corn kernels, drained, roughly chopped
- 1 medium zucchini, grated
- 1 small carrot, grated
- 2/3 cup grated cheddar cheese
- 1/3 cup panko breadcrumbs
- 1 1/2 tbsp Vegemite Squeezy
- 1 green onion, chopped
- 1 garlic clove, crushed
- 3 sheets frozen puff pastry, partially thawed, halved
- 1 egg, lightly beaten
- Sesame seeds, to sprinkle
- Sweet chilli sauce, to serve
- Select all ingredients

Directions:

1. Place chicken mince, corn kernels, zucchini, carrot, cheddar cheese, panko breadcrumbs, Vegemite Squeezy, green onion and garlic in a bowl. Season with pepper. Mix well to combine.
2. Place 1 pastry half on a flat surface. Spoon 1/3 cup mince mixture along 1 long side of pastry. Brush

edges with egg. Roll up from long side to form a log. Trim ends. Cut into 4 equal pieces. Repeat with remaining pastry, mince mixture and egg.

3. Brush tops of rolls with egg and sprinkle with sesame seeds. Line air fryer with baking paper, leaving a 1cm border to allow air to circulate. Cook on 200C, in batches, for 13 to 15 minutes or until golden and cooked through. Stand for 5 minutes. Serve with sweet chilli sauce.

Recipe Notes
VEGEMITE contains vitamins B1, B2, B3 and folate. Enjoy as part of a balanced, varied diet and active lifestyle.

Air Fryer Chicken Legs

Servings: 4

Cooking Time: 30 Minutes

Ingredients:
- 3-4 chicken legs
- 1 tablespoon olive oil
- 1 tablespoon chicken seasoning* see note
- ½ teaspoon garlic powder
- salt & pepper to taste

Directions:
1. Preheat air fryer to 370°F.
2. Pat chicken dry with a paper towel. Drizzle olive oil over chicken legs and generously season with chicken seasoning, garlic powder, and salt & pepper to taste.
3. Place the chicken legs in a single layer in the air fryer basket, skin side down, and cook for 20 minutes.
4. Flip the legs over and cook an additional 5-10 minutes or until the legs reach 165°F.

Notes
*Premade chicken seasonings can vary in flavor and salt level. Season to taste or preference.
Homemade Chicken Seasoning
1 teaspoon paprika
1/2 teaspoon garlic powder
1/2 teaspoon kosher salt, more or less to taste
1/4 teaspoon black pepper
1/4 teaspoon dried thyme leaves
Ensure legs aren't too crowded so air can circulate around them. Do not overlap.

Air Fryer Turkey Breast

Servings: 6

Cooking Time: 50 Minutes

Ingredients:
- 1 (4-to 6-pound) bone-in, skin on turkey breast with ribs removed* or 1 (3-pound) boneless roast**
- 2 tablespoons extra-virgin olive oil
- 2 cloves garlic minced
- 2 teaspoons kosher salt
- 2 teaspoons chopped fresh rosemary leaves
- 2 teaspoons chopped fresh sage leaves
- 1 teaspoon chopped fresh thyme leaves
- 1/2 teaspoon freshly ground black pepper
- 1 teaspoon Dijon mustard
- Mushroom Gravy optional for serving

Directions:
1. Remove the turkey from the refrigerator and let stand at room temperature for 30 minutes. With paper towels, pat the turkey very dry.
2. When ready to cook, preheat the air fryer to 350 degrees F for at least 5 minutes. In a small bowl, whisk together the oil, garlic, salt, rosemary, sage, thyme, black pepper, and mustard until evenly blended.
3. Rub all over the turkey.
4. Place the turkey in the air fryer basket, skin-side down (see notes if using a turkey with the ribs still attached). Cook for 20 minutes, then slide out the basket and carefully flip the turkey over.
5. Continue cooking for 30 to 50 minutes more, until an instant read thermometer inserted at the thickest part of the meat without touching bone registers 155 degrees F (poultry is considered cooked per the FDA at 165 degrees F, but its temperature will rise as it rests. DO NOT OVERCOOK or it will be dry). Boneless turkey breast in the netting will take longer than bone-in turkey breast without netting. Remove the turkey to a cutting board and cover with foil. Let rest at least 15 minutes.
6. To carve, cut each side of the breast away from the bone by running a large, sharp knife along and down each side of the breast bone using long, even strokes. Continue down the breast, following along the whole bone.

7. Lift the meat away in one large piece, then place it flat on the cutting board and cut crosswise into slices.
8. Repeat on the other side of the breast. Pull the remaining meat away from the bone and slice. Serve hot or at room temperature.

Notes

*If using bone-in turkey breast, be sure your air fryer is at least 5 quarts (my 5.5-quart air fryer can fit a turkey that is up to 5-pounds).

*I prefer to use a breast with the ribs removed, because it more easily fits in the air fryer AND I find it turns out more moist, because it can lay flat with the breast bone touching the bottom of the air fryer and cook more quickly and evenly. That said, if you can only find a turkey breast with the ribs still attached and don't want to remove them yourself, you can still make this recipe. To cook, lay the breast on its side (this is likely the only way it will fit in your basket) and cook for 25 minutes. Flip over to the other side and continue cooking until the breast reaches 155 degrees F at the thickest part. I also recommend brining a breast with the ribs attached to help keep it moist during cooking (see Dry Brine and Wet Brine for recipes).

**If using a boneless breast, such as a 3-pound Butterball breast, remove the outermost plastic netting and wrapper from the roast. Leave the inner string netting on (this holds the roast together as it cooks). It will take longer to cook than a bone-in breast because of how snugly it is held together.

TO STORE: Refrigerate turkey breast in an airtight storage container for up to 3 days.

TO REHEAT: Wrap turkey in an aluminum foil pouch and rewarm gently in a baking dish in the oven at 350 degrees F, drizzling some broth over the top before sealing the foil pouch and placing it in the oven.

TO FREEZE: Freeze leftovers in an airtight, freezer-safe storage container for up to 3 months. Let thaw overnight in the refrigerator before reheating.

Air Fryer Buffalo Chicken Zucchini Skins

Servings: 8

Cooking Time: 10 Minutes

Ingredients:
- 2 large zucchini (about 9 ounces each)
- olive oil spray
- 1/2 teaspoon salt
- 1/4 teaspoon garlic powder
- 1/4 teaspoon paprika
- Buffalo Chicken Stuffing:
- 7 ounce shredded skinless chicken breasts (from rotiserie chicken or make in slow cooker)
- 1 ounces 1/3 less fat cream cheese (softened)
- 1/4 cup Franks hot sauce (plus more for drizzling on top)
- 4 teaspoons crumbled blue cheese or gorgonzola
- 1/4 cup light Blue Cheese or Ranch Dressing
- 2 tablespoons chopped scallions

Directions:
1. Combine the cream cheese and hot sauce together in a medium bowl until smooth. Add the chicken.
2. Cut zucchini in half lengthwise; then cut in half to give you 8 pieces. Scoop out the pulp on each piece, leaving a 1/4-inch shell on all sides (save pulp for another use).
3. Place zucchini skins on a work surface. Spray both sides with olive oil then season both sides with salt, then cut side with garlic powder and paprika.
4. Cook 350F in batches for 8 minutes, until tender-crisp. Place 3-4 tablespoons buffalo chicken inside each skin and top with 1/2 teaspoon cheese, dividing equally. Cook until cheese is melted, about 2 minutes longer. Serve right away each drizzled with 1/2 tablespoon blue cheese dressing topped with scallions for garnish. Serve hot.

Air Fryer Chicken Parmesan

Servings: 4

Cooking Time: 10 Minutes

Ingredients:

- 4 small chicken breasts or 2 large ones, halved
- 1 large egg
- 1 cup panko breadcrumbs
- 1 teaspoon salt
- 1/2 teaspoon pepper
- 1 tablespoon Italian seasoning
- 1 cup marinara sauce
- 1/2 cup mozzarella cheese
- 1/2 cup parmesan cheese

Directions:

1. Preheat the air fryer to 190C/375F. Grease the air fryer basket.
2. Pound the chicken breasts until they are around half an inch thick.
3. In one bowl add the egg and whisk it well. In the second bowl, add the panko, salt, pepper, and Italian seasoning.
4. Dip the chicken in the egg then dip it in the dry mix until fully coated. Repeat the process until all four chicken breasts are breaded.
5. Add the chicken into the greased air fryer basket and air fry for 9 minutes, flipping halfway through.
6. Remove the air fryer basket and add 1/4 cup of marinara sauce on top of each chicken breast. Sprinkle the parmesan cheese and mozzarella cheese on top.
7. Place the air fryer basket back in the air fryer and air fry for a further 2-3 minutes, or until the cheese melts.

Notes

TO STORE: Place leftovers in an airtight container and store them in the refrigerator for up to five days.

TO FREEZE: Wrap it in foil or use an air-tight container and store the chicken parm in the freezer for up to 6 months.

TO REHEAT: Reheat them in the air fryer for 2-3 minutes, or until the cheese is sizzling.

Air Fryer Chicken Drumsticks

Servings: 6

Cooking Time: 13 Minutes

Ingredients:

- 6 chicken drumsticks
- 2 teaspoons baking powder
- 1 teaspoon smoked paprika
- 2 teaspoons Italian seasonings
- 1 teaspoon garlic powder
- 1 teaspoon onion powder
- 1 teaspoon brown sugar
- 2 tablespoons olive oil

Directions:

1. Preheat the air fryer to 200C/400F.
2. In a small bowl, add the spices and mix well.
3. Pat dry the chicken drumsticks. Toss the drumsticks through the spice mix then drizzle the oil all over.
4. Place the drumsticks in the air fryer basket and cook for 8 minutes, flip, and cook for a further 6-8 minutes, or until cooked and crispy.
5. Serve immediately with your favorite sides.

Notes

TO STORE: Leftovers can be stored in an air-tight container in the refrigerator for 4-5 days.

TO FREEZE: Air fryer chicken drumsticks can be frozen in a ziplock bag for up to 3 months.

TO REHEAT: Either microwave them for 20-30 seconds or reheat in the air fryer until crispy.

Actually Crispy Oven Baked Wings

Servings: 4

Cooking Time: 40 Minutes

Ingredients:

- 1 ½ pounds chicken wings split and tips removed, about 18 wings
- 1 tablespoon flour
- 1 teaspoon baking powder
- ½ teaspoon seasoned salt
- ½ teaspoon black pepper
- 1 tablespoon olive oil

Directions:

1. Pat wings dry with a paper towel.
2. Prepare a pan by lining with foil and placing a baking rack on it. Spray the rack with cooking spray.
3. Combine flour, baking powder, salt and pepper. Toss with wings and place on prepared pan. Refrigerate 30 minutes (or up to 4 hours) uncovered.
4. Preheat oven to 425°F.
5. Toss wings with olive oil in a bowl (ensuring there are no dry spots of flour) and return back to the prepared pan.
6. Bake wings 20 minutes, flip and bake an additional 15 minutes. If your wings are smoking, remove the foil and add new foil. Cook until crisp and broil 1 minute each side if desired.
7. Toss with sauce or serve with dips.

Notes

Pat the wings dry, moisture makes them steam (not crisp).

Don't skip the resting period, this allows them to dry out and to draw moisture from the skin.

Toss with olive oil for a little bit of crisp without the deep fry.

Place on a rack on your baking pan, this allows air to circulate all around the wings.

Line the pan with foil for easy clean up. If the pan begins to smoke from the drippings, add a new sheet of foil on top of the old foil.

For an extra-crisp, put the baked wings under the broiler for about 2 minutes until the skins start to become golden brown.

Air Fryer Sweet And Sour Chicken

Servings: 2

Cooking Time: 10 Minutes

Ingredients:

- FOR THE CHICKEN
- 1 pound chicken breasts or chicken thighs, cut into 1 1/2 to 2-inch chunks
- 2 tablespoons cornstarch (or potato starch)
- FOR THE SWEET AND SOUR SAUCE
- 1 cup pineapple juice
- 1/2 cup brown sugar
- 3 tablespoons rice wine vinegar
- 1 tablespoon soy sauce
- 1/4 teaspoon ground ginger (or 1 teaspoon freshly grated ginger)
- 2 tablespoons cornstarch
- 2 tablespoons water
- OPTIONAL
- 1/4 cup pineapple chunks
- 3-4 drops of red food coloring (for traditional orange look)

Directions:

1. Preheat air fryer to 400 degrees.
2. Combine chicken pieces and cornstarch into a bowl and mix until the chicken is just fully coated.
3. Place chicken in the air fryer and cook for 7-9 minutes, shaking the basket halfway through. Then remove from the air fryer.
4. Meanwhile, mix together the pineapple juice, brown sugar, rice wine vinegar, soy sauce, and ginger and bring to a simmer for 5 minutes. Stir occasionally.
5. Mix together the cornstarch and water in a separate bowl to create a "slurry" then add it to the sweet and sour sauce along with pineapple chunks and red food coloring (if using).
6. Let simmer for one more minute then remove sauce from the heat.
7. Toss chicken and sauce together and serve alongside rice or veggies for a full meal.*

Notes

* sauce makes enough to help coat veggies or rice to serve alongside.

How to Reheat Sweet and Sour Chicken in an Air Fryer:

Cook chicken in a preheated air fryer at 350 degrees for 3 to 4 minutes until warmed thoroughly.

If chicken is already coated with sauce, place chicken on an air fryer pan to help with the mess.

Air Fryer Bbq Chicken Legs

Servings: 3

Cooking Time: 30 Minutes

Ingredients:

- 1 pound chicken legs (drumsticks or thighs-separated)
- 2 Tablespoons oil
- 2 Tablespoons BBQ sauce (or sugar-free bbq sauce for keto)
- 1 Tablespoon Worcestershire sauce
- 1/2 teaspoon salt , or to tase
- 1/4 teaspoon fresh crack black pepper , or to taste
- EQUIPMENT
- Air Fryer

Directions:

1. In bowl combine oil, bbq sauce, Worcestershire sauce, salt and pepper. Add chicken and stir to completely coat with in the marinade. Cover and marinate for about 20 minutes.
2. Pre-heat air fryer at 360°F/182°C for about 4 minutes. Spray the air fryer basket with oil or use an air fryer perforated parchment sheet. Place chicken in air fryer
3. Air Fry at 360°F/182°C for about 25-30 minutes, depending on the thickness of the drumsticks or thighs. Turn the chicken after cooking for 15 minutes.
4. Once cooked, let the chicken cool a bit and enjoy!

Notes

Air Frying Tips and Notes:

Shake or turn at least once while cooking. Don't overcrowd the air fryer basket.

If cooking in a non-preheated air fryer, it take longer to cook than if the Air Fryer is already pre-heated. Recipe timing is based on pre-heating the air fryer.

Recipes were tested in 3.4 to 6 qt air fryers. If using a larger air fryer, the recipe might cook quicker so adjust cooking time.

Remember to set a timer to shake/flip/toss as directed in recipe.

Teba Shio Chicken Wings

Servings: 3-4

Ingredients:

- ¾ cup cooking sake
- 1 pound chicken wings
- 1 teaspoon kosher salt
- 2 teaspoons Shichimi togarashi, plus more for serving
- ¼ teaspoon freshly ground white pepper
- 1 teaspoon grapeseed oil
- ½ teaspoon lemon juice
- Oil spray
- Lemon wedges, for serving

Directions:

1. Place the sake and chicken wings into a resealable plastic bag.
2. Marinate the chicken wings in the refrigerator for 20 minutes, ensuring they are fully submerged.
3. Remove the chicken wings and pat dry with paper towels.
4. Season the wings with salt, Shichimi togarashi, white pepper, grapeseed oil, and lemon juice.
5. Select the Preheat function on the Air Fryer, adjust temperature to 380°F, then press Start/Pause.
6. Spray the preheated inner basket with oil spray, then place the chicken wings into the preheated air fryer.
7. Select the Chicken function, adjust time to 18 minutes, press Shake, then press Start/Pause.
8. Flip the chicken wings halfway through cooking. The Shake Reminder will let you know when.
9. Remove when done and serve with Shichimi togarashi and lemon wedges.

Air Fryer Turkey Burgers

Servings: 4

Cooking Time: 14 Minutes

Ingredients:

- 1 pound ground turkey
- 1 tablespoon olive oil
- 1 egg yolk
- 3 tablespoons seasoned bread crumbs
- 1 teaspoon onion powder
- 1 tablespoon Worcestershire sauce
- ½ teaspoon salt or to taste
- ⅛ teaspoon pepper or to taste
- ¼ cup barbecue sauce divided
- For Serving
- 4 hamburger buns
- lettuce, tomatoes, pickles, onions

Directions:

1. Preheat air fryer to 350°F.
2. Combine all ingredients in a bowl except barbecue sauce in a bowl.
3. Divide the mixture into four ½" thick patties and place in the air fryer in a single layer.
4. Brush the turkey burgers with half of the barbecue sauce. Cook for 6 minutes. Flip burgers and brush with remaining barbecue sauce. Return to air fryer and cook for an additional 5-8 minutes until burgers have reached 165°F.
5. Serve on buns with desired toppings.

Notes

Turkey patties should reach (165°F) on an instant-read thermometer.

Air Fryer can vary by brand, check your patties early to ensure they do not overcook.

When placing the patties in the Air Fryer, use your thumb to create a small indent in the middle of the patties. This will help them cook evenly and keep them from bulging in the middle.

FISH & SEAFOOD RECIPES

Chipotle Tuna Melt

Ingredients:

- 1 can (5 ounces) tuna
- 3 tablespoons La Costeña Chipotle Sauce
- 4 slices white bread
- 2 slices pepper jack cheese

Directions:

1. SELECT Preheat on the Air Fryer, adjust to 320°F, and press Start/Pause.
2. MIX the tuna and chipotle sauce until combined.
3. SPREAD half of the chipotle tuna mixture onto each of 2 bread slices.
4. ADD a slice of pepper jack cheese onto each and top with the remaining 2 bread slices, making 2 sandwiches.
5. PLACE the sandwiches into the preheated air fryer.
6. SELECT Bread, adjust time to 8 minutes, and press Start/Pause.
7. CUT diagonally and serve.

Air Fryer Tuna Melts

Ingredients:

- 12 oz tuna
- 2 dil pickles
- 1/4 medium onion
- 1/4 cup mayonnaise
- Garlic Powder
- Black Pepper
- Bread of choice
- 4 slices of american cheese

Directions:

1. In a large bowl mix together your tuna, pickles, onion, mayonnaise, garlic powder, and black pepper.
2. Top 4 of the slices of bread with the tuna mixture and add a slice of cheese to each.
3. Toast at 400 degrees for 5 minutes
4. Carefully remove from the air fryer and enjoy!

Air Fryer Coconut Shrimp

Servings: 4

Cooking Time: 10 Minutes

Ingredients:

- 1 lb large shrimp peeled
- 2 large eggs
- 1 cup unsweetened coconut flakes
- 1/2 cup panko bread crumbs
- 1/2 cup all-purpose flour
- 1/2 teaspoon garlic powder
- 1/2 teaspoon smoked paprika
- 1/2 teaspoon salt
- 1/2 teaspoon pepper

Directions:

1. Preheat the air fryer to 180C/350F.
2. In a bowl, beat the eggs. In a separate bowl, combine the coconut flakes with the bread crumbs. In a third bowl, add the flour, smoked paprika, salt, pepper, and garlic powder.
3. Dip the shrimp in the flour, shake off excess, then the egg mixture, and then in the coconut and panko mixture, pressing firmly for it to stick. Repeat the process.
4. Grease the air fryer basket, then add the coconut shrimp to it, ensuring that they are not touching one another.
5. Air fry for 10-12 minutes, flipping halfway through.
6. Once the shrimp are golden brown, remove them from the air fryer basket and serve immediately.

Notes

TO STORE: Keep the air fried coconut shrimp in an airtight container in the fridge for up to 3 days.

TO FREEZE: Once they're cooked and cooled to room temperature, place them in an airtight container and freeze for up to 2 months.

TO REHEAT: Place the chilled or frozen coconut shrimp in the air fryer and reheat until warmed through.

Air Fryer Breaded Fish Fillets Recipe

Ingredients:

- 100g cod fillets
- 40g breadcrumbs
- 1 large egg, beaten
- 2 tbsp plain flour
- 1 tbsp Parmesan cheese
- 1 tsp dried basil
- Salt and pepper, to taste

Directions:

1. Add the flour to a bowl and coat the cod fillets.
2. In another bowl, mix together the breadcrumbs, Parmesan, basil, salt and pepper.
3. Dip the fillets in the beaten egg, then coat in the breadcrumb mixture.
4. Spray the fish with oil on all sides, then place in a 190°C air fryer and cook for 15-20 minutes until golden brown.

Air Fryer Shrimp Cocktail

Servings: 6

Cooking Time: 10 Minutes

Ingredients:

- FOR THE SHRIMP
- 1 pound (455 g) raw shrimp , deveined and shells removed
- 1 teaspoon (5 ml) oil , to coat shrimp
- salt , to taste
- black pepper , to taste
- SHRIMP COCKTAIL SAUCE
- 1/2 cup (120 g) ketchup (or low-carb tomato sauce for keto)
- 2 teaspoons (10 ml) Worcestershire sauce
- 1 teaspoon (5 ml) prepared horseradish
- 1 teaspoon (5 ml) fresh lemon juice
- 1/4 teaspoon (1.25 ml) celery salt
- 1/4 teaspoon (1.25 ml) garlic powder
- 1/4 teaspoon (1.25 ml) salt , or to taste
- black pepper to taste
- fresh lemon slices
- 1 (1) small cucumber , sliced (optional)
- fresh herbs for garnish (optional)
- EQUIPMENT
- Air Fryer

Directions:

1. In bowl, combine ketchup, Worcestershire sauce, horseradish, fresh lemon juice, celery salt, garlic powder, salt and black pepper. Stir until well mixed then set aside.
2. After shrimp shells are removed and de-veined, rinse and pat dry the shrimp. Coat shrimp with oil, and then season with salt and pepper. Place the shrimp in the air fryer basket or tray in a single layer.
3. Air Fry shrimp at 400°F for 8-12 minutes, or until cooked through. Shrimp comes in different sizes so check halfway through to make sure it's cooked enough or to your liking. After air frying, let the shrimp cool completely and chill in the fridge until ready to serve.
4. Serve the cooked shrimp with the shrimp cocktail sauce and slices of fresh lemon and cucumbers. Garnish with fresh herbs if you are feeling fancy.

Air Fryer Coconut Shrimp With Orange-soy Dipping Sauce

Servings: 6

Cooking Time: 15 Minutes

Ingredients:

- FOR THE COCONUT SHRIMP
- 1 lb. (454 g) large shrimp , peeled and deveined
- 1/2 teaspoon (2.5 ml) smoked paprika
- 1/2 teaspoon (2.5 ml) garlic powder
- salt , to taste
- black pepper , to taste
- 1/3 cup (42 g) flour
- 2 eggs
- 1/2 cup (43 g) sweetened coconut flakes
- 1/2 cup (54 g) bread crumbs
- FOR THE DIPPING SAUCE:
- 1/4 cup (80 g) orange marmalade
- 1 Tablespoon (15 ml) chili garlic sauce , or to taste
- 1 Tablespoon (15 ml) rice vinegar
- 1 teaspoon (5 ml) soy sauce
- EQUIPMENT
- Air Fryer

Directions:

1. Rinse and pat dry the shrimp. Season all sides of shrimp with paprika, garlic powder, salt and pepper.

2. You'll need 3 bowls: In first bowl, add the flour. In second bowl, whisk together eggs. In third bowl combine coconut flakes and bread crumbs. Coat shrimp in flour mixture, then dip in egg mixture, then coat the shrimp with the coconut/bread crumb mixture.

3. Coat the air fryer basket/tray with oil spray. Lay the coated shrimp in a single layer (cook in batches if needed). Lightly spray coated shrimp with oil.

4. Air Fry at 380°F for about 10-14 minutes or until the crust is golden brown, flipping after 8 minutes if needed for even cooking. Cooking times will vary depending on shrimp size.

5. For the Dipping Sauce: Whisk together the all of the dipping sauce ingredients (marmalade, chili garlic sauce, rice vinegar, and soy sauce) until smooth. Set aside until ready to serve with the coconut shrimp.

Air Fryer Crab Rangoon

Servings: 7

Cooking Time: 10 Minutes

Ingredients:

- 5 ounces cream cheese
- 5 ounces crab meat
- 2 green onions, chopped
- 1 teaspoons worcestershire
- 1 1/2 teaspoons minced garlic
- salt and pepper to taste
- olive oil cooking spray
- 28 wonton wrappers
- water

Directions:

1. In a medium bowl, combine the cream cheese, crab meat, green onions, worcestershire, minced garlic and salt and pepper.

2. Place one wonton wrapper on a cutting board. Use a brush to brush the edges of the wrapper with water.

3. Fill the center of the wrapper with 1 ½ teaspoons of crab mixture.

4. Grab two opposite corners of the wrapper to come together in the middle to make a triangle. Then take the other ends and bring them to the middle as well.

Press to make sure you get all the air out and seal the seams together.

5. Spray the bottom of your air fryer. Then place your crab rangoons in the basket. Spritz the tops of the rangoons with a little more cooking spray.

6. Bake at 360 for 10 minutes, Checking at the 5 minute mark and then every 2 minutes after, to check on how brown and crispy you want them. Depending on your air fryer brand and size, cooking time varies slightly. Serve with sweet chili sauce.

Air Fryer Fish & Chips

Servings: 4

Cooking Time: 1 Hour 10 Minutes

Ingredients:

- Chips
- 2 russet potatoes
- 2 tablespoons olive oil
- ½ teaspoon seasoned salt
- Fish
- 1 ½ pounds cod fillets or other white fish
- 1 cup pancake mix dry
- ½ cup buttermilk
- 1 egg
- 1 cup panko bread crumbs
- ½ teaspoon seasoned salt
- ½ teaspoon old bay seasoning
- ½ teaspoon salt and pepper each
- ½ teaspoon paprika

Directions:

1. Chips
2. Scrub potatoes and cut into ¼" fries.
3. Place fries in a large bowl of cold water and soak for 30 minutes. Drain well and dab dry.
4. Toss fries with oil and salt.
5. Preheat the air fryer to 390°F.
6. Place the potatoes in the basket and cook for 10 minutes. Shake the potatoes and cook an additional 6-8 minutes or until crisp. Remove from the air fryer and place on a plate.
7. Fish
8. While fries are cooking, prepare fish. Place pancake mix in a shallow bowl.

9. Combine buttermilk and egg in a second bowl and combine bread crumbs and seasonings in a third bowl.
10. Dab fish dry with a paper towel. Dip in egg mixture and then into pancake mixture.
11. Dip back into the egg mixture and then into the bread crumbs. Spray generously with cooking spray.
12. Once the fries are removed, add fish to the air fryer and cook at 390°F for 12 minutes or until cooked through and flaky. Do not overcook.
13. Add fries back to the air fryer and cook 1-2 minutes to heat through.

Notes

Ensure fish is fully thawed before you begin or it will not crisp properly.

Fish cook time can vary based on thickness.

Thicker fries may need more time, thinner fries may need a bit less time. Appliances can vary but it is easy to check on the fries a couple of minutes early and add more time if needed.

To Make More Fries cook several smaller batches. Once ready to serve, add all fries to the air fryer basket and cook at 390°F for 2-3 minutes or until heated through.

Grain-free Tuna Cat Treats

Servings: 50

Cooking Time: 4 Hr

Ingredients:

- 1 can tuna, packed in water (5 ounces)
- 1 egg white
- Items Needed
- Food processor or blender
- Hand mixer
- Parchment paper
- Piping bag with small star nozzle attachment
- Parchment paper
- Piping bag with small star nozzle attachment

Directions:

1. Drain the canned tuna well and place the drained tuna in a food processor or blender. Set aside.
2. Place the egg white in a large mixing bowl. Using a hand mixer, beat the egg white until stiff peaks form.
3. Place 2 tablespoons of the whipped egg white in with the tuna. Blend thoroughly until the mixture is a smooth paste.
4. Remove the tuna paste mixture and gently fold into the remaining whipped egg white.
5. Transfer the mixture to a piping bag with a small star nozzle attachment.
6. Line the Food Dehydrator trays with parchment paper.
7. Pipe the mixture into small rounds on the parchment paper-lined trays.
8. Set temperature to 145°F and time to 4 hours, then press Start/Stop.
9. Remove the treats when done and crispy and crunchy. Cool completely, then serve to your pet.

Lemon-pepper Air-fryer Shrimp And Veggies

Servings: 2

Ingredients:

- 10 ounce fresh or frozen extra-large shrimp in shells, thawed if frozen, peeled, and deveined
- 2 lemons
- 1 tablespoon olive oil
- 1 teaspoon salt-free lemon-pepper seasoning, such as Mrs. Dash
- ¼ teaspoon salt
- ¼ teaspoon garlic powder
- ¼ teaspoon paprika
- 1 small zucchini, halved lengthwise and sliced 1/4 inch thick
- 2 medium carrots, sliced

Directions:

1. Thaw shrimp if frozen. Rinse shrimp; pat dry. Preheat air fryer at 400°F.
2. Squeeze 3 Tbsp. juice from one of the lemons; cut the remaining lemon into wedges. In a large bowl combine lemon juice and the next five ingredients (through paprika). Add shrimp, zucchini, and carrots; toss to coat.
3. Using a slotted spoon, transfer shrimp mixture to air-fryer basket. Cook 9 to 11 minutes or until shrimp are opaque, stirring occasionally. Serve with lemon wedges.

Air Fryer Lobster Tails With Lemon-garlic Butter

Servings: 2

Cooking Time: 10 Minutes

Ingredients:

- 2 (4 ounce) lobster tails
- 4 tablespoons butter
- 1 teaspoon lemon zest
- 1 clove garlic, grated
- salt and ground black pepper to taste
- 1 teaspoon chopped fresh parsley
- 2 wedges lemon

Directions:

1. Preheat an air fryer to 380 degrees F (195 degrees C).
2. Butterfly lobster tails by cutting lengthwise through the centers of the hard top shells and meat with kitchen shears. Cut to, but not through, the bottoms of the shells. Spread tail halves apart. Place tails in the air fryer basket with lobster meat facing up.
3. Melt butter in a small saucepan over medium heat. Add lemon zest and garlic; heat until garlic is fragrant, about 30 seconds.
4. Transfer 2 tablespoons of butter mixture to a small bowl; brush this onto lobster tails. Discard any remaining brushed butter to avoid contamination from uncooked lobster. Season lobster with salt and pepper.
5. Cook in the preheated air fryer until lobster meat is opaque, 5 to 7 minutes.
6. Spoon reserved butter from the saucepan over lobster meat. Top with parsley and serve with lemon wedges.
7. Tips
8. You can use frozen lobster tails, just thaw them first before proceeding with instructions.

Seafood Paella

Servings: 3-4

Cooking Time: 1 Hr

Ingredients:

- 2 teaspoons extra-virgin olive oil
- ½ tablespoon garlic, minced
- ½ yellow onion, small diced
- 1 teaspoon kosher salt, plus more to taste
- ¼ teaspoon saffron or ½ teaspoon turmeric
- 1 teaspoon paprika
- ½ cup tomatoes, diced
- 1 cup plus 2 tablespoons chicken broth
- 2 bay leaves
- 1 cup medium grain white rice, rinsed and drained
- ½ cup frozen green peas
- 7 large shrimps (31/35 size), peeled and deveined
- 8 clams
- 7 mussels
- Parsley, chopped, for garnish
- 1 lemon, sliced into wedges, for serving
- Items Needed
- Small stock pot with lid

Directions:

1. Set Mode to Sauté on the Rice Cooker, adjust time to 20 minutes, then tap Start.
2. Add the oil to the pot, then add the garlic and onions and cook until aromatic.
3. Add the salt, saffron or turmeric, paprika, tomatoes, and chicken broth into the pot and bring to a simmer.
4. Add in the bay leaves and rice, then mix to combine. Tap Cancel when done.
5. Select the White Rice function, set to Med/Short, then tap Start.
6. Open the lid when 8 minutes remain on the timer and mix in the frozen peas, then add the shrimp on top and close the lid to continue cooking.

Air Fryer Bacon Wrapped Scallops

Servings: 4

Cooking Time: 20 Minutes

Ingredients:

- 16 large sea scallops (cleaned and pat dry with paper towels)
- 8 slices center cut bacon
- 16 toothpicks
- olive oil spray
- freshly ground black pepper (to taste)

Directions:

1. Preheat air fryer to 400F 3 minutes.
2. Place the bacon in the air fryer to partially cook 3 minutes, turning halfway. Remove and set on a paper towel to cool.
3. Remove any side muscles on the scallops. Pat the scallops dry with paper towels to remove any moisture.
4. Wrap each scallop in slice of bacon and secure it with a toothpick.
5. Spritz olive oil over scallops and season lightly with black pepper.
6. Arrange scallops in a single layer in the air fryer, cook, in batches 8 minutes turning halfway until scallop is tender and opaque and bacon is cooked through. Serve hot.

Air Fryer Salmon

Servings: 4

Cooking Time: 10 Minutes

Ingredients:

- Nonstick spray
- 4 (4- to 5-ounce) skin-on salmon fillets
- 1 tablespoon olive oil
- 1 teaspoon lemon pepper (or 1/2 teaspoon black pepper and 1 teaspoon fresh lemon zest)
- 1/2 teaspoon kosher salt
- 1/4 teaspoon black pepper
- Lemon wedges, for garnish

Directions:

1. Prepare the air fryer basket:
2. Lightly spray the inside of the air fryer basket with nonstick cooking spray.
3. Season the salmon:

4. Place the salmon on a plate skin side down. Drizzle the tops (the skinless sides) with olive oil and season with lemon pepper, salt, and black pepper.
5. Air fry the salmon:
6. Place the salmon in the air fryer basket. Make sure they aren't touching. I like to place mine skin-side down, but skin-side up is also an option. If you'd like, place a few lemon slices under each piece of salmon.
7. Air fry the salmon for about 8 minutes at 350°F. The salmon is done when it reaches an internal temperature of 135°F to 140°F when measured with an instant read thermometer. You can cook it longer if you want a slightly more well-done piece.
8. Serve the salmon:
9. Serve the salmon with fresh lemon wedges for squeezing on top.
10. Refrigerate leftover salmon for up to 3 days.

Air Fryer Salmon Flatbreads

Servings: 4

Ingredients:

- 1 tbsp. red wine vinegar
- 2 tbsp. olive oil, divided
- 1 tbsp. capers, chopped
- 2 scallions, 1 finely chopped and 1 thinly sliced
- Kosher salt and pepper
- 1 pt. grape tomatoes
- 1 lb. skinless salmon filet, cut into 11/2 inch pieces
- 1 tbsp. chopped flat-leaf parsley
- Labneh or Greek yogurt, for serving
- 4 pieces naan or flatbread, warmed
- 2 c. baby arugula or kale
- Sliced scallion, for serving
- Crumbled feta, for serving

Directions:

1. In small bowl, combine red wine vinegar, 1 tablespoon olive oil, capers, chopped scallion, and 1/4 teaspoon pepper; set aside.
2. Heat air fryer to 400°F. In bowl, toss tomatoes and remaining tablespoon oil with 1/4 teaspoon each salt and pepper. Season salmon with 1/4 teaspoon each salt and pepper.
3. Place salmon in single layer on 1 side of air fryer and add tomatoes to remaining space (piling them

is great). Air-fry until salmon is just barely opaque throughout, 6 minutes.

4. Transfer tomatoes to bowl with vinegar-scallion mix and toss to combine, then toss with parsley.

5. Spread labneh or yogurt on flatbreads, top with salmon and arugula, then spoon tomato mixture on top. Sprinkle with sliced scallions and crumbled feta if desired.

Teriyaki-glazed Salmon

Servings: 4

Ingredients:

- 1 1/2 lb. salmon fillet
- Kosher salt and pepper
- 1/2 c. Honey-Lime Teriyaki Sauce, divided
- 1/4 c. rice vinegar
- 1 tsp. honey
- 1/2 tsp. grated peeled fresh ginger
- 1 shallot, thinly sliced
- 2 Persian cucumbers, thinly sliced
- Cilantro, for sprinkling

Directions:

1. Heat oven to 400°F. Place salmon on foil-lined baking sheet, season with 1/4 teaspoon salt, then spoon 3 tablespoons teriyaki sauce on top and roast 10 minutes. Spoon remaining teriyaki sauce over top and continue roasting 8 minutes.

2. Increase heat to broil. Baste salmon with any sauce that has fallen to sides of pan and broil until sticky and opaque throughout, 2 to 4 minutes.

3. Meanwhile, in bowl, whisk together vinegar, honey, and 1/4 teaspoon each salt and pepper to dissolve. Stir in ginger then shallot and let sit 5 minutes. Add cucumber and let sit, tossing occasionally, 10 minutes. Transfer salmon to platter and, with slotted spoon, spoon cucumber mixture over top and sprinkle with cilantro.

4. AIR FRYER DIRECTIONS:

5. Remove the insert from air-fryer basket. Heat air-fryer to 400°F. Place a sheet of aluminum foil on top of the insert and place salmon on top of that. Season with 1/4 teaspoon salt. Drizzle with 2 tablespoons teriyaki sauce. Return the insert (with the salmon) to air-fryer basket and air-fry, basting every 5 minutes with any sauce that has fallen to

sides of salmon (and additional sauce if necessary), until opaque throughout and sticky on top, 15 to 18 minutes.

Air-fryer Breaded Shrimp

Servings: 4

Cooking Time: 10 Minutes

Ingredients:

- 1/2 cup all-purpose flour
- 1/2 teaspoon seafood seasoning
- 1/2 teaspoon dill weed
- 1/2 teaspoon pepper
- 1 large egg
- 1/2 cup 2% milk
- 1 teaspoon hot pepper sauce
- 1 cup panko bread crumbs
- 1 pound uncooked shrimp (26-30 per pound), peeled and deveined
- Cooking spray
- Optional: seafood cocktail sauce and lemon wedges

Directions:

1. Preheat air fryer to 375°. In a shallow bowl, mix flour, seasoned salt, dill weed and pepper. In a separate shallow bowl, whisk egg, milk and hot pepper sauce. Place bread crumbs in a third shallow bowl. Dip shrimp in flour to coat both sides; shake off excess. Dip in egg mixture, then in bread crumbs, patting to help adhere.

2. In batches, arrange shrimp in a single layer in greased air fryer; spritz with cooking spray. Cook until lightly browned and shrimp turn pink, 3-4 minutes on each side. If desired, serve with cocktail sauce and lemon wedges.

Air Fryer Catfish

Servings: 4

Cooking Time: 22 Minutes

Ingredients:
- 1 pound catfish fillets
- 1 cup fish fry breading I prefer Louisiana brand
- 1 small lemon cut into wedges
- 1 Tablespoon olive oil

Directions:
1. Preheat the Air Fryer to 400 degrees Fahrenheit for 5 minutes.
2. Rinse and dry the catfish with a paper towel before coating.
3. Add the seasoned breading to a shallow bowl and then dip each piece of fish until coated completely. Spray the sides of each fillet with olive oil spray.
4. Place fillets in the prepared Air Fryer basket in a single layer. Cook at 400°F for 10 minutes, then carefully flip the catfish filets and cook for an additional 10 minutes.
5. Flip once more and cook for an additional 1-2 minutes to get them extra crispy if desired.
6. Serve with coleslaw and tartar sauce. Squeeze fresh lemon juice over the filets just before serving.

Notes

NOTE: This recipe was made using a 1700 watt 5.8 qt Basket style Cosori Air Fryer. Your brand of air fryer may cook differently depending on the size and the power of the air fryer. Use this recipe as a guide when using a different brand of air fryer.

Laying a piece of parchment paper in the Air Fryer makes cleaning up super easy. After cooking, all you have to do is remove the parchment paper from the Air Fryer! There's no greasy residue left, making cleaning up super quick and painless!

To ensure your fish has a crunchy crust, make sure you tap some of the excess breading off, so the fish isn't too bready. In addition, Use spray oil instead of olive oil, so the fish isn't too soggy.

Baked Salmon With Garlic And Dijon

Servings: 4

Cooking Time: 15 Minutes

Ingredients:
- 1 1/2 lb salmon filet
- 2 Tbsp fresh parsley, chopped
- 2 Tbsp light olive oil, not extra virgin
- 2 Tbsp fresh lemon juice
- 3 garlic cloves, pressed
- 1/2 Tbsp Dijon mustard
- 1/2 tsp salt, we use sea salt
- 1/8 tsp black pepper
- 1/2 Lemon, sliced into 4 rings

Directions:
1. Preheat oven to 450°F and line a rimmed baking sheet with silpat or foil. Slice salmon into 4 portions and arrange them on a lined baking sheet, skin-side-down.
2. In a small bowl, combine: 2 Tbsp parsley, 2-3 pressed cloves garlic, 2 Tbsp oil and 2 Tbsp lemon juice, 1/2 Tbsp Dijon, 1/2 tsp salt, and 1/8 tsp pepper.
3. Generously spread the marinade over the top and sides of the salmon then top each piece with a slice of lemon.
4. Bake at 450°F for 12-15 min or until just cooked through and flaky. Don't over-cook.

Recipe Notes

Air Fryer Salmon: place salmon pieces on the wire basket, spread marinade over the top and air fry at 450°F for 6-7 minutes or just until cooked through.

Air Fryer Cod

Servings: 4

Cooking Time: 8 Minutes

Ingredients:

- 4 fillets cod 4 ounces each
- 2 tablespoons olive oil divided
- 1/4 cup basil finely chopped
- 1/2 teaspoon salt
- 1/4 teaspoon pepper

Directions:

1. Preheat the air fryer to 200C/400F.
2. Pat dry the fish then add it to a bowl and drizzle one tablespoon of olive oil on top.
3. In a small bowl, whisk together the remaining olive oil, basil, salt, and pepper.
4. Rub the basil mixture over the fish.
5. Grease the air fryer basket. Add a single layer of cod fillets to it.
6. Air fry for 8-9 minutes, flipping halfway through.

Notes

TO STORE: Place leftovers in a shallow container and store them in the refrigerator for up to five days.

TO FREEZE: Let the fish cool completely then transfer them to a shallow container and store them in the freezer for up to two months.

TO REHEAT: You can reheat it in the air fryer or microwave.

New England Baked Cod

Ingredients:

- 2 fillets cod
- 1 cup butter-flavored crackers
- 2 Tbsp parsley, minced
- 1 Tbsp Parmesan, grated
- 1 tsp Auntie NoNo's Everything Seasoning
- 1 Tbsp lemon juice
- 1 Tbsp lemon zest
- 3 Tbsp unsalted butter, melted

Directions:

1. In a bowl, mix together the crackers, parsley, Parmesan, Auntie NoNo's Everything Seasoning, lemon juice and zest to make the topping.
2. Add in half of the melted butter.
3. Pat dry the cod fillets and spread on the remaining melted butter.

4. Season the cod to taste. We used some more Auntie NoNo's Everything Seasoning.
5. Spoon on the cracker mixture on top of the fish and press down as best as possible. Some of the mixture will fall off, but just do your best to get as much on the top.
6. Transfer the fish to the air fryer basket.
7. Air fry at 350°F for about 13 minutes, or until your fish reaches an internal temperature of 145°F.
8. Finish them off with some more lemon juice and enjoy!!

Dorito-crumbed Fillets

Servings: 4

Ingredients:

- 4 Vegetarian Quorn Fillets
- 150ml buttermilk (or sub for 130ml/4.55fl. oz milk + 1 tbsp apple cider vinegar)
- 90g tangy cheese tortilla chips (1/2 a sharing bag)
- 1 egg
- 30g plain flour
- Salt & pepper
- To serve salsa
- COOKING MODE
- When entering cooking mode - We will enable your screen to stay 'always on' to avoid any unnecessary interruptions whilst you cook!

Directions:

1. Place the Quorn Fillets in a large bowl. Cover with buttermilk. Cover and place in the fridge for 4 hours or overnight to marinate
2. Preheat one zone of your Ninja Foodi Dual Zone Air Fryer to 180°C. Line a baking tray with baking paper
3. Place the tortilla chips in a food processor and pulse until coarsely chopped. Transfer to a plate
4. Crack the egg into a shallow bowl and whisk. Place the flour, a pinch of salt & pepper on a separate plate and mix
5. Drain the Quorn, discarding the buttermilk. Place the Quorn on the flour and roll a few times to coat. Dip in the egg, then in tortilla chips, pressing firmly to coat. Transfer to the prepared tray

6. Place the fillets in the air fryer, select Air Fry, and set time to 10 minutes, Select Start/Stop and fry until golden and cooked through

7. Transfer to a serving platter. Serve with salsa & Mexican style rice

Air Fryer Shrimp Tempura

Servings: 4

Cooking Time: 30 Minutes

Ingredients:
- 1 pound fresh jumbo shrimp
- 1 ¼ cups all-purpose flour, divided
- ½ cup cold water
- 2 egg whites (or 1 large egg), beaten
- ⅓ cup cornstarch
- ½ teaspoon salt

Directions:
1. Prepare the shrimp by deveining them (if necessary) and removing the shell up to the tail. Make 4-5 small notches on the "belly" of each shrimp and stretch them out. Pat them dry with paper towels.

2. In a bowl, whisk together ½ cup of the flour, water, and egg whites. In a second bowl, add the remaining flour.

3. Place cornstarch and salt in a plastic zipper bag. Add shrimp and toss well to coat.

4. Preheat the air fryer to 370 degrees F for 5 minutes. Spray the inner basket generously with cooking oil spray.

5. Dip shrimp, one at a time, in the wet flour batter, then dredge them through the dry flour to lightly coat them. Place them on a clean plate or parchment-lined baking sheet.

6. Working in batches, set the shrimp in the basket in a single, uncrowded layer. Spray them well with cooking oil spray, then air fry for 7-8 minutes, until lightly golden.

7. FROM FROZEN:

8. Prep shrimp through step 5, then place the plate or baking sheet in the freezer for 1 hour to flash-freeze. Remove the shrimp and store in a plastic zipper bag until ready to cook.

9. When ready to cook, preheat the air fryer to 370 degrees F for 5 minutes. Spray the inner basket with cooking oil spray.

10. Working in batches, set the frozen shrimp in the basket in a single, uncrowded layer. Spray them well with cooking oil spray, then air fry for 12-15 minutes, until lightly golden.

Notes
HOW TO REHEAT SHRIMP TEMPURA:
Preheat your air fryer to 370 degrees.
Place shrimp in air fryer basket and cook for 3-5 minutes or until hot.

Cornflake Crusted Salmon And Lemon Cardamom Veg

Servings: 4

Ingredients:
- For the lemon cardamom veg
- 75g almonds
- 2 tbsp coconut oil
- 3 cloves garlic (peeled, finely chopped)
- 6 Seeds of cardamom pods
- 3/4 tsp sea salt
- 1 medium head of broccoli (approx. 350g, cut into florets)
- 200g shredded cavolo nero
- 1 Zest and juice of lemon
- For the cornflake crusted salmon
- 4 salmon fillets (roughly 130g each)
- 4 tbsp mayonnaise
- 2 tbsp whole grain mustard
- 1/4 tsp garlic granules
- 1/4 tsp onion granules
- Pinch sea salt
- 100g gluten-free cornflakes
- Cooking spray
- COOKING MODE
- When entering cooking mode - We will enable your screen to stay 'always on' to avoid any unnecessary interruptions whilst you cook!

Directions:

1. Add the almonds to zone 1 drawer, without the crisper plate installed. Select Zone 1, then turn the dial to AIR FRY and set the temperature to 180°C and the time to 6 minutes. Press START/STOP to begin cooking. Shake the almonds halfway through cooking then transfer to a plate and leave to cool down before roughly chopping.

2. In a small bowl stir together the mayonnaise, mustard, garlic granules, onion granules and sea salt until combined. Divide equally between the salmon fillets, spreading over the tops and sides.

3. Crush the gluten-free cornflakes by hand or place them into a ziplock bag and bash with a rolling pin until you get a coarse crumb. Spoon over the salmon fillets and gently pat until coated evenly.

4. Insert the crisper plate into the zone 2 drawer and spray with cooking spray. Place the salmon fillets into the drawer and close.

5. Add the coconut oil, chopped garlic, and cardamom seeds to the zone 1 drawer and close. Select Zone 1, then turn the dial to AIR FRY and set the temperature to 180°C and the time to 8 minutes. Press MATCH, then START/STOP to begin cooking.

6. After 1 minute add the sea salt and broccoli florets to the zone 1 drawer, shake or stir, then close the drawer and cook for 5 minutes before adding the shredded cavolo nero.

7. When the unit has finished cooking add the chopped toasted almonds, lemon juice and zest to the zone 1 and stir. Serve the salmon and vegetables immediately and enjoy.

Air Fryer Shrimp

Servings: 4

Cooking Time: 5 Minutes

Ingredients:

- 1 lb large shrimp raw; remove shell and tail if desired; note 1
- 1 1/2 tablespoons olive oil
- 1 1/2 tablespoons lime juice note 2
- 1 1/2 tablespoons honey note 3
- 2 cloves garlic minced
- 1/8 teaspoon salt
- To garnish
- lime wedges
- cilantro

Directions:

1. Marinade - In a large bowl, stir together the olive oil, lime juice, honey, garlic and salt. Add the shrimp and marinate for 20-30 minutes.

2. Cook - Heat the air fryer to 390°F/200°C.Shake excess marinade off the shrimp and put the whole batch in the air fryer.

3. Cook for 2 minutes, give the basket a good shake, and return to the air fryer. Cook for another 2-3 minutes, or until shrimp are pink and cooked through.

4. Serve - with lime wedges and cilantro.

Notes

you can use any type of shrimp and adjust the cook time as needed. Make sure you start with fully thawed shrimp; we do recommend peeling, deveining, and removing the tails to make them easier to eat.

fresh limes add an extra punch of flavor, but bottled can be used; lemon may be swapped in a pinch

honey may be swapped for maple syrup or your favorite liquid sweetener

Storage

This recipe is best served fresh, however, the marinade can be stirred together up to 4 days ahead and stored in the fridge. Do not marinate shrimp for more than 1 hour.

SANDWICHES & BURGERS RECIPES

Chick-fil-a Crispy Chicken Sandwich Copycat

Servings: 4

Cooking Time: 10 Minutes

Ingredients:

- 4 chicken breast halves
- 1/2 cup pickle juice
- 1/4 cup water
- 1/2 cup milk
- 1 large egg
- oil for frying
- 4 hamburger buns
- Pickle, lettuce, tomato and cheese slices , for topping
- For the breading:
- 1 cup all-purpose flour
- 3 Tablespoons powdered sugar
- 1/2 teaspoon paprika
- 1 teaspoon freshly ground black pepper
- 1/2 teaspoon chili powder
- 1/2 teaspoon salt
- 1/2 teaspoon baking powder
- 1-2 teaspoons cayenne pepper *optional, for a spicy chicken sandwich
- For the Chick-fil-A-sauce
- 1/2 cup mayonnaise
- 1 teaspoon dijon mustard
- 3 teaspoons yellow mustard
- 2 teaspoon barbecue sauce (hickory tastes the best)
- 2 Tablespoons honey
- 1/2 teaspoon garlic powder
- 1/2 teaspoon paprika
- 1 teaspoon lemon juice

Directions:

1. Marinate the chicken: combine the pickle juice and water in a ziplock bag. Add the chicken breast halves and marinate for 30 minutes.
2. Make the sauce: Make the Chick-fil-A sauce by combining all ingredients in a bowl. Mix well and set aside.
3. Next, in a large bowl mix the breading ingredients together: flour, powdered sugar, paprika, black pepper, chili powder, salt, and baking powder.
4. In another bowl mix the milk, and egg.
5. Add 2-3 cups of oil to a large saucepan and heat oil to about 350 degrees F.
6. Coat the chicken: Dip the marinated chicken into the egg mixture, and then coat in the flour breading mixture. Now "double-dip" by repeating this step and dipping that same chicken tender back into the egg mixture and then back into the flour again!
7. Pan fry: Place chicken in hot oil and fry for 3-4 minutes on each side. Remove to paper towel to dry.
8. Assemble Sandwich: Toast the sandwich buns. Grab the Chick-fil-A sauce and smooth it on both sides of the buns. Top with lettuce, cheese, and crispy chicken! Enjoy!

Notes

Air Fryer Chick-Fil-A Sandwich:

Preheat fryer to 370°F. Grease the inside basket/rack of the air fryer and place two coated chicken breasts in the air fryer. Lightly spray the top of the chicken. Cook the chicken for 11-13 minutes, flipping halfway through cook time. Assemble sandwich as instructed below.

Baked Chick-Fil-A Sandwich:

Preheat oven to 450°F. Place a wire cooling rack on top of a baking sheet. Place your coated chicken breasts on the wire rack and spray both sides lightly with olive oil. Bake the chicken for 12 minutes, flip and bake for another 15 minutes or until it's cooked through.

For a Spicy Chick-Fil-A Chicken Sandwich:

We love spicy chicken at our house! If you'd like to add a little heat to your chicken sandwich, add 1-2 teaspoons of cayenne pepper to the flour mixture when making the breading. I like to coat my kids sandwiches in the flour first, then add the cayenne for spice, and make mine and my husbands.

Air Fried Peanut Butter And Jelly Sandwich

Servings: 2

Cooking Time: 4 Minutes

Ingredients:

- 2 Tablespoons butter melted
- 4 Tablespoons peanut butter
- 4 Tablespoons grape jelly
- 4 slices bread

Directions:

1. Prepare the air fryer basket with a nonstick cooking spray such as avocado oil or olive oil.
2. Take each slice of bread and butter one side of the bread.
3. Add peanut butter to one piece of bread and jelly to the other piece of bread.
4. Add the peanut butter and jelly together, and place them in a single layer in your prepared air fryer basket.
5. Use the air fry function and fry the sandwiches at 400 degrees Fahrenheit for 3-4 minutes, flipping the sandwich halfway through the cooking time.
6. Remove the sandwich from the air fryer and serve immediately.

Notes

This recipe was made with a basket style 5.8 qt Cosori air fryer. If you are using a different brand of air fryer, you may need to adjust the cooking time accordingly. All air fryers cook a little differently, and it's always best to check a recipe by making a test run so you can adjust the cooking time as needed.

Use your favorite jam or favorite jelly that you and your family love, but also consider going outside of the box with this pb&j sandwich.

I love to use the class white bread, but you can also use wheat bread or sourdough bread or any of your favorite pieces of bread with this recipe.

Sunny Side Burgers

Servings: 4

Ingredients:

- Oil spray
- 2 teaspoons kosher salt
- 1 teaspoon ground black pepper
- ½ teaspoon onion powder
- ½ teaspoon garlic powder
- 1 pound ground angus beef
- 4 sunny side up fried eggs, with runny yolks
- 4 slices Munster cheese, or cheese of choice
- 2 cups caramelized onion
- 2 tablespoons mayonnaise
- 4 Brioche burger buns, sliced
- Boston bib lettuce, as needed
- Tomato slices, as needed
- 2 teaspoons crushed red pepper flakes, for garnish
- Ketchup, for serving
- Yellow mustard, for serving

Directions:

1. Combine the kosher salt, ground black pepper, onion powder, and garlic powder together in a large bowl. Mix the spices into the ground angus beef and then form into four quarter pound patties, about a ½-inch thick.
2. Place the cooking pot into the base of the Indoor Grill, followed by the grill plate.
3. Select the Air Grill function on max heat, adjust the temperature to 510F and cooking time to 7 minutes, press Shake, then press Start/Pause.
4. Note: This will yield a medium-rare burger.Spray the grill grate lightly with oil spray once the grill is done preheating.
5. Place the burger patties onto the preheated grill grate and press Start/Pause. Flip the patties when the Shake reminder beeps.
6. Add the cheese to the patties when 2 minutes remain on the timer.
7. Remove when done and set onto a wire rack to rest.
8. Spread the mayonnaise over the insides of the sliced Brioche buns.
9. Select the Broil function, adjust time to 3 minutes, press the Preheat button to cancel the automatic preheat, then place the buns mayonnaise side down

onto the grill plate. Press Start/Pause then close the lid to begin cooking.

10. Remove the buns when toasted and set aside until cool to the touch.

11. Assemble the burgers by topping the bottom halves of the brioche buns with lettuce and tomato, then place the burger patty on top followed by caramelized onions, then the sunny side up fried egg, sprinkle with crushed red pepper flakes, and finish with the top half of the bun.

12. Serve immediately with the condiments on the side and pair with hashbrowns or home fries, and fresh fruit.

Air Fryer Hamburgers

Servings: 4

Cooking Time: 12 Minutes

Ingredients:

- 4 hamburger patties

Directions:

1. Preheat the Air Fryer to 370 degrees Fahrenheit. Prepare the Air Fryer basket with nonstick cooking spray.

2. Add the hamburger patties into the Air Fryer basket in a single layer.

3. Cook in the preheated fryer for 6 minutes. Flip the hamburger patties and cook for an additional 5-7 minutes, depending on how well done you would like the hamburgers.

4. Carefully remove the hamburger patties from the Air Fryer basket and serve with your favorite sides and toppings.

Notes

If cooking frozen hamburger patties, add an extra minute or two to the cook time to ensure they are cooked thoroughly.

Air Fryer Salmon Fish Sandwich

Servings: 4

Cooking Time: 10 Minutes

Ingredients:

- Lemon-Caper Mayo:
- 6 tbsp mayonnaise (I like Sir Kensington)
- 2 tablespoons drained capers (minced)
- 2 teaspoons fresh lemon juice
- For the Fish:
- 16 ounces skinless salmon fillet (if frozen thawed, cut in 4 pieces)
- 1 teaspoon kosher salt (divided)
- 2 large egg whites (lightly beaten)
- 1 cup seasoned panko* (or gluten free panko)
- Olive oil spray
- 4 whole wheat buns (or gluten free buns)
- 4 butter lettuce leaves

Directions:

1. Combine the ingredients for the Lemon-Caper Mayo in a small bowl and refrigerate until ready to eat.

2. Pat the salmon dry with a paper towel. Cut the fish into 4 pieces, about 4 x 4 inches. Season with 1/2 teaspoon salt.

3. Place the egg whites in a shallow bowl.

4. In a second shallow bowl combine the panko with remaining 1/2 teaspoon salt.

5. Dip the fish into the egg whites, then the panko. Set aside.

6. Spray the basket with oil. Lay the fish on the basket in a single layer, in batches as needed.

7. Spray the tops of the fish with oil and air fry 400F 8 minutes, turning half way, until golden and crisp.

8. Serve fish on buns with lettuce and divide the sauce.

Notes

No air fryer, no problem! Bake in a preheated oven 400 12 to 14 minutes, turning halfway.

*NOTE 1/4 CUP GETS TOSSED AFTER

Check labels for gluten-free.

Best Ever Grilled Cheese Sandwiches

Servings: 2

Ingredients:

- 2 tablespoons mayonnaise
- 1 teaspoon Dijon mustard
- 4 slices sourdough bread
- 2 slices Swiss cheese
- 2 slices cheddar cheese
- 2 slices sweet onion
- 1 medium tomato, sliced
- 6 cooked bacon strips
- 2 tablespoons butter, softened

Directions:

1. Combine mayonnaise and mustard; spread over 2 bread slices. Layer with cheeses, onion, tomato and bacon; top with remaining bread. Spread outsides of sandwiches with butter.
2. In a small skillet over medium heat, toast sandwiches until cheese is melted, 2-3 minutes on each side.

Air Fryer Cheeseburgers

Servings: 4

Cooking Time: 30 Minutes

Ingredients:

- 500 grams minced beef
- 1 egg
- ¾ cup (75g) panko breadcrumbs
- 2 tablespoons barbecue sauce
- 1 tablespoon smoked paprika
- 1 clove garlic, crushed
- ¼ cup (70g) low-sugar tomato sauce
- 4 large brioche buns (400g)
- olive oil cooking spray
- 4 slices cheddar
- 4 centre-cut bacon rashers (140g)
- 2 tablespoons whole-egg mayonnaise
- 4 baby cos lettuce leaves
- 1/3 cup (40g) burger pickles
- to serve: sweet potato chips

Directions:

1. Using your hands, combine beef, egg, breadcrumbs, barbecue sauce, paprika, garlic and 1 tablespoon of the tomato sauce in a large bowl, then season; mix well. Shape mixture into four patties the same size as the brioche buns; ensure they will all fit into the air fryer basket. Spray all over with cooking spray.
2. Preheat a 7-litre air fryer to 180°C/350°F for 3 minutes.
3. Spray the air fryer basket with cooking spray. Taking care, place patties in the basket; at 180°C/350°F, cook for 10 minutes, turning halfway through cooking time, or until browned and cooked through. Transfer to a plate and top each with a slice of cheddar; cover loosely with foil to keep warm.
4. Arrange bacon in the air fryer basket. Reset the temperature to 200°C/400°F; cook for 5 minutes until crisp.
5. Split and toast brioche buns. Spread bun bases with mayonnaise, then top with lettuce, patties, bacon, pickles and remaining tomato sauce; sandwich together with bun tops.
6. Serve cheeseburgers with sweet potato chips.

Air Fryer Burgers

Servings: 4

Cooking Time: 12 Minutes

Ingredients:

- 1 lb ground hamburger recommend 85/15
- 1 tsp Worcestershire sauce
- 1 tsp seasoning salt
- 1 tsp garlic powder
- 1 tsp onion powder
- 4 slices cheese
- 4 buns
- *additional toppings like lettuce tomatoes, pickles, bacon ketchup, mustard. mayonnaise etc.

Directions:

1. In a large mixing bowl combine hamburger, Worcestershire sauce, seasoning salt, garlic powder and onion powder and combine with hands. Do not overmix. Form into 4 patties.
2. Place the burgers in the air fryer, you may have to cook two at a time depending on the size of your air fryer.
3. Cook the burgers for 8 minutes at 360 degrees F. Flip the burgers over and cook for an additional 6-8 minutes or until the internal temperature of the burgers are 160 degrees F.
4. Top each burger with a slice of cheese and cook for an additional minute or until the cheese is melted.
5. Serve on buns with your favorite condiments.

Notes

Press a thumbprint into the middle of each patty before it goes in the air fryer. This will help the patty hold it's shape rather than shrinking as it cooks.

Air Fryer Frozen Burgers

Servings: 4

Cooking Time: 15 Minutes

Ingredients:

- 4 beef burger patties

Directions:

1. There is no need to preheat the air fryer for this and no oil needed too, simply place the frozen burger patties in the air fryer.
2. Cook the burgers for 15 minutes at 180C/360F flipping once for even cooking. If you would be topping the burger with cheese, add it 30 seconds or 1 minute before the end of the cooking time and cook until the cheese melts. I mostly do 30 seconds.
3. If cooking thinner patties then cook for 10 minutes at180C/360F. The internal temperature of well done burger should register 160F/71C
4. Carefully remove the cooked burger from the air fryer basket and assemble on hamburger buns with other toppings of choice. Enjoy!
5. PS: the burger shrinks when cooked so don't be alarmed if this happens

Notes

Estimated nutritional value provided for hamburger patties only.